CW01431329

ONCE UPON a RHYME

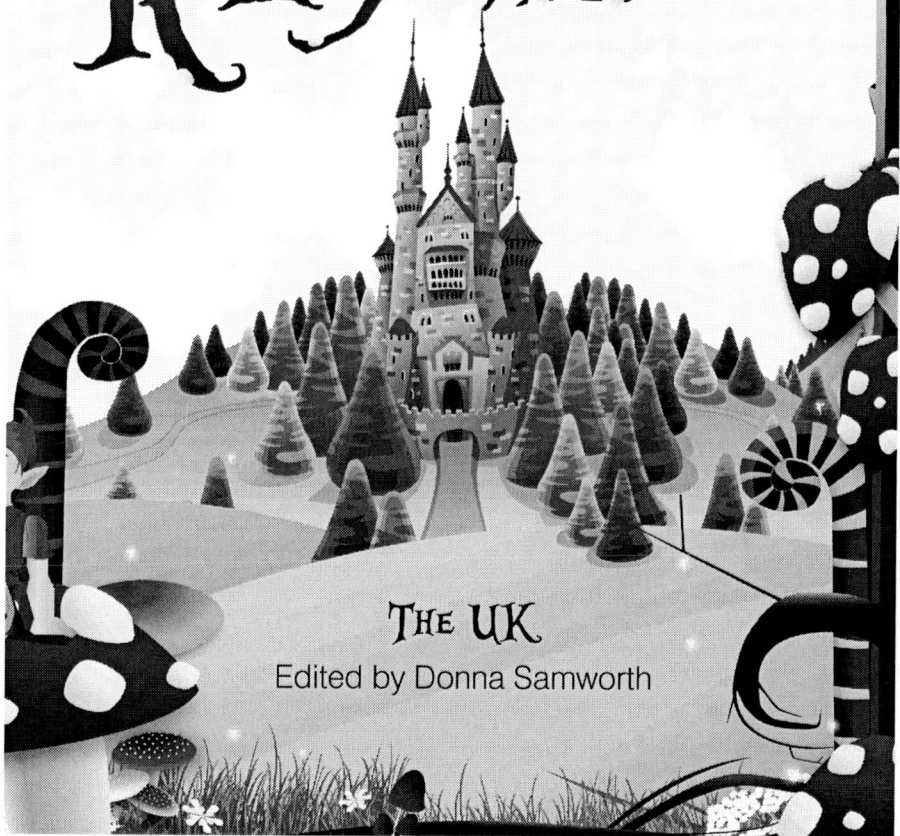

THE UK

Edited by Donna Samworth

First published in Great Britain in 2011 by:

Young**Writers**

Remus House
Coltsfoot Drive
Peterborough
PE2 9BF
Telephone: 01733 890066
Website: www.youngwriters.co.uk

THIS BOOK BELONGS TO

....

FOREWORD

Here at Young Writers our objective is to help children discover the joys of poetry and creative writing. Few things are more encouraging for the aspiring writer than seeing their own work in print. We are proud that our anthologies are able to give young authors this unique sense of confidence and pride in their abilities.

Once Upon A Rhyme is our latest fantastic competition, specifically designed to encourage the writing skills of primary school children through the medium of poetry. From the high quality of entries received, it is clear that Once Upon A Rhyme really captured the imagination of all involved.

The resulting collection is an excellent showcase for the poetic talents of the younger generation and we are sure you will be charmed and inspired by it, both now and in the future.

CONTENTS

MADDIE STEWART IS OUR FEATURED POET THIS YEAR. SHE HAS WRITTEN a NONSENSE WORKSHOP FOR YOU aND INCLUDED SOME OF HER GREaT POEMS. YOU CaN FIND THESE IN THE MIDDLE OF YOUR BOOK.

THE POEMS

Love

Love is like a stream of water,
It tastes like fresh, sweet, pure honey,
It smells like the magnificent smell of roses,
It looks like people being as one,
It feels like you're never unhappy,
Forever as one!

Princess Obayori (8)

The Man

Over the hills, there is a man
Riding on a horse, his name is Dan.
In the silence of the night
Were the horse's footsteps, in the dim light.

In his view he saw a cottage near,
And when coming to a halt he started to hear
Two men talking, each holding a gun,
While the man waited to pounce when the time had come.

When he opened the door he saw a girl
Strapped onto a chair, screaming for help.
Without thinking, he ran to untie the tie,
But ended up with life saying goodbye.

Over the hills, there was a man
Riding on his horse, his name was Dan.
In the silence of the night
Were the horse's footsteps, in the dim light.

Joshua Obayori (10)

Rhymes Of Mine

Jump on the tyres to get the wires,
Jump on the fence and land on the bench,
Jump on the trampoline,
Onto the shed to be happy and funny,
Jump on the car and drive on the giraffe.
Because you'll need some apples,
Climb up the tree,
Act like a monkey,
Hang upside down.

Bobby How (7)

Swinter Swonderland

S ummer and winter combined together
W ill you join me
I n this wonderland?
N o one's getting colder
T ill winter actually comes
E veryone joining in throwing snowballs at the bin
R unning up the hill with my friend Bill.

S ummer's nearly gone
W inter's on its way
O ur holidays are nearly finished
N ow we're ready to go back to school
D one playing, it's time to work
E veryone getting their uniforms on
R unning to school
L ike a cheetah chasing a deer
A ll getting snugly in school as warm as toast
N early the next month
D ecember's nearly gone.

Daniel Hedges (9)
Arundale Community Primary & Nursery School, Hyde

Seasons

Winter is a winter dream,
With a cold and snowy theme,
Snow is fun,
When I'm wrapped up under the icy sun.

Lambs are bleating,
Farmers keeping,
Blooming blossom,
Hopping possum.

Sun is shining,
Whilst I'm dining,
Ice cream
Golden gleam.

Watch the leaves falling,
While my mother's calling,
Boom, crackle, pop,
As fireworks drop.

Paris Lawrie & Chloe Louise Smith (10)
Arundale Community Primary & Nursery School, Hyde

My Dreams

In my dreams anything can happen,
Sometimes I imagine I'm in the forest with my sister,
The stream absorbing the sunlight,
I could go on forever,
Bird watching in the sun,
Everlasting happiness rushing through the air,
But then,
Reality wanders upon me, I hopelessly awake,
My next dream patiently awaiting me.

Megan Ghadiali (10)
Arundale Community Primary & Nursery School, Hyde

A Night Of Fright!

Witches, warlocks, ghostly ghouls,
One night a year
Break all the rules.
Pictures on posters come to life,
People scared when the clock strikes midnight!
Candles glow in the pumpkin's head,
Faces so deadly it fills you with dread!
They lie in wait for passers-by
Or swoop down low from darkened sky.
A cracking branch, the misty air,
The ghosts and ghouls are everywhere.

Katie May Stubbs (8)
Astwood Bank First School, Redditch

Autumn's Coming

A corns dropping off the trees like bombs
U nfolding blankets for icy nights
T iny icicles may be small but they're cold
U nderneath the leaves lie grass as green as green
M agically, animals start to disappear
N ights get icy, frosty and cold

Autumn's coming and it's rather magical!

Ellie-Mae Vickridge (8)
Astwood Bank First School, Redditch

Autumn Is Here

A utumn is here,
U p for hot chocolate,
T rees' leaves falling down,
U p on the sofa, watching TV,
M illions of stars in the sky,
N ight-times getting darker.

Thomas Gant (8)
Astwood Bank First School, Redditch

Halloween

H aunting lots of kids,
A ll the children in costumes,
L istening to wolves howling,
L ooking at a full moon,
O ut trick or treating,
W ind blowing loud,
E njoying lots of candy,
E vil ghosts scaring,
N ight sky twinkling.

Olivia Dutton (9)
Astwood Bank First School, Redditch

Halloween

H alloween, people trick or treating
A nyone should be sleeping in their comfy beds
L ollies being licked
L ovely candy being eaten
O nly trick or treaters out in the dark
W ings of fake bats on show
E very parent and trick or treater's awake
E very child excited about the candy
N aughty boys eating lots of sweets before dinner!

Jonathan Bryan (8)
Astwood Bank First School, Redditch

Incredible Autumn

A ir is cold
U nravel the cooking pot, sticking toffee apple
T wisting, turning, I feel the tingle of the water bottle
U nwinding clocks so sleep in, sleep in
M y animals hibernating
N ow hear crackling fire and sip hot chocolate

A ll hear the roar of fireworks
N ow hear all the leaves gliding to the floor
D awn, dark squirrels hunt

H ear spiky conkers drop
A ll rain, no sun!
R ather cold, doesn't stop trick or treating
V ests are on, no short sleeves!
E veryone steps on crispy leaves
S oups to keep us warm
T oday is pumpkin decorating day!

Amelia Melville-Green (8)
Astwood Bank First School, Redditch

Hairy, Scary Nights Of Halloween

H airy, scary beasts bring treats.
A skeleton jumps right at you.
L uscious tastes of sweets.
L iving with all the frights.
O n a dark night, foggy mist comes out.
W ill a ghost really come out?
E at sweets all night.
E nd the lovely bright days of summer love.
N ights are really scary, coldness gives you a fright.

Thomas Best (8)
Astwood Bank First School, Redditch

Halloween Night

H owling dogs
A nxious people
L oud cat yowling
L ight burning
O ften hearing doors slam
W hining babies
E ating sweets
E vening's turning black
N oisy adults, having fun!

Victoria-Rose Slaler (8)
Astwood Bank First School, Redditch

Halloween

H earing people screaming,
A lways in October,
L ooking for houses,
L ights shining,
O utfits people wear,
W ind blowing in the air,
E njoying the night,
E vil people knocking on doors,
N ails scratching on people.

Shelby Houghton (8)
Astwood Bank First School, Redditch

Halloween

Halloween, sugar mice
Sugar mice, very nice
Candyfloss, nice to lick
Even when the big clock ticks
Zombies run, house to house
Jelly beans bounce
And monsters pounce
Sweets are treats
On trick or treat night
Ghosts and ghouls fight
In the pitch-black night . . .

Eleanor Foster (8)
Astwood Bank First School, Redditch

Fireworks

B right glow sticks glowing in the dark
O nions sizzling on the pan
N oisy people around the fire
F lowing wind
I n the night sky stars are shining
R oaring fire crackling loudly
E xploding fireworks

N ight sky flashing and glowing
I gnite the rockets, hear the scream
G lowing sparklers
H ot dogs so tasty
T ired children ready for bed!

Maisie Adams (8)
Astwood Bank First School, Redditch

Bonfire Night

Smell the fire with burning flames
Feel the coldness pinching your face
Crunching of candy apples
Laughter of little children
Dazzling fireworks
Bright colours in the sky
Banging, popping, it's a surprise.

Kiera Keane (9)
Astwood Bank First School, Redditch

Bonfire Night

Bone-chilling sounds of Bonfire Night,
Crackling of the fire,
Crunch of a candy apple,
Zooming of a rocket into the starry sky,
Feel of the warm fire glow,
The shouts and screams of children winning prizes,
Chill of a breath,
Misty smoke rising from the fire,
Smell of hot dogs burning,
Bangs and dazzling colours and lights.

Tobin Walsh (8)
Astwood Bank First School, Redditch

Autumn And Harvest

A ir is cold and silent
U nravelling blankets of corn and wheat
T ime to collect the veg, fruit and harvest
U se the heaters to keep you warm
M any animals hibernating
N ew seasons creeping up on us

I t's time to keep warm for the winter
S quirrels collecting acorns and nuts

F amilies huddling warm and dry
U nwinding curtains to brown daylight
N ow winter's almost here.

Michael Beldham (9)
Astwood Bank First School, Redditch

Autumn Is Here

Trees are getting bolder,
Bolder as every second comes,
Animals hunting for food and friends
Just as winter comes,
Nights getting colder and colder
Just as moonlight is getting brighter.

Harry Keen (9)
Astwood Bank First School, Redditch

What Is Bonfire Night?

B urning food
O lives
N uts so warm
F ires blazing
I gniting fireworks to the sky
R ockets screaming
E yes so bright

N ights so cold
I ce cream
G uy Fawkes remembered
H eights of lights
T ights so warm

Bonfire Night!

Maisie Bash (8)
Astwood Bank First School, Redditch

Amazing Autumn

A utumn is arriving
U nfold icy roads
T urn summer into autumn
U s people feeling cold
M illions of birds flying to hot countries
N ot many people about

I feel so cold
S ome people stay inside, keeping warm

A million animals hibernating
R ed leaves fluttering down
R ed and grey squirrels hunting for nuts
I t's turning freezing cold
V ital snow, freezing people
I n autumn most trees looking blank
N ow it's freezing all outside
G irls and boys playing in snow.

William Beldham (9)
Astwood Bank First School, Redditch

Bonfire Night Is Here

All the fireworks up in the sky
Zooming, banging, swirling, whizzing around
The smell of toffee apples
The crackling of the dazzling fire
This is why I like Bonfire Night
A very historical night indeed.

Henry Hemming (8)
Astwood Bank First School, Redditch

Autumn Nights

When I looked out of my window
I saw nothing but steam
And a spider on the ceiling
Oh I can smell my hot soup waiting
Oh I *love* this autumn night
Watching TV
But the best bit is when
We're snuggling on the sofa
Now I'm not so chilly.

Emily Green (8)
Astwood Bank First School, Redditch

All About Autumn

Harvest leaves falling down,
In every city and every town.
All the tractors in the fields,
Collecting up the farmers' yields.
All the nights are turning cold,
The winter months start to unfold.
Cuddled up in our house,
Hearing squeaks of a tiny mouse.
In the distance all around,
Autumn's here, all golden and brown.

Myles Hulland (8)
Astwood Bank First School, Redditch

Bonfire Night

Entering a firework show,
Often hearing people saying, 'Oo, ah.'
I stare at fireworks.
Refusing to go to bed.
Bonfire smoke nearly making people faint.
Next morning old fireworks laying.

Daniel Martin (8)
Astwood Bank First School, Redditch

Harvest

H ear spiky hedgehogs rustling on crunchy dry leaves.
A pples falling from bare trees.
R abbits eating orange, big, juicy carrots.
V ery fat, seeded pumpkin.
E choing very loud bird sounds.
S ilky, sparkly webs from big spiders.
T he shy, furry squirrels going hunting for nuts.

Joshua Monroe (8)
Astwood Bank First School, Redditch

Harvest

H earing the rattling leaves that are crunchy brown like chocolate.
A utumn is a lovely month of the year because it is becoming cold and frosty.
R estful days, everyone sleepy and quiet.
V ery windy days in autumn can nearly blow you over.
E vening sunshine in the sky.
S ilky seeds in the ground waiting till springtime.
T urning leaves from green to red, slowly falling off the trees.

Josie Steele (8)
Astwood Bank First School, Redditch

Autumn

A magnificent tree with five thousand leaves
U nder the ground badgers hibernate
T he animals start to collect food for the winter
U p in the trees squirrels hunting for nuts
M oney-like leaves fall off the trees
N ightingales flying away to South Africa.

Ryan Benson (8)
Astwood Bank First School, Redditch

Harvest

H ear the rustling of the wind blowing the trees.
A nimals creeping on the gold crunchy ground looking for food.
R eflections in the cold, misty, dark, deep pond.
V egetables being carefully picked by farmers.
E ating the lovely juicy fruit and vegetables for our lunch.
S ilky spiderwebs hanging from ceilings.
T alking about food, the farmers' harvest for us to eat.

James Whitehouse (8)
Astwood Bank First School, Redditch

Harvest

H ear the rustling leaves swishing from side to side
A nimals finding food before they hibernate
R ed squirrels collecting nuts
V egetables very tasty for our tea
E choing forests bouncing wind off the trees
S ilky leaves waving in the autumn breeze
T asty apples falling onto the frosty ground.

Joe Hamilton (8)
Astwood Bank First School, Redditch

Leaves

L ovely colourful leaves make a carpet on the ground
E njoy walking on the crunchy colours
A utumn, shiny red
V ans picking all of the flowers
E verything tasty when the sun rises
S ilky seeds growing on the ground.

Daniel Wright (8)
Astwood Bank First School, Redditch

Harvest

H earing the rustling leaves when the trees shake in the wind
A nimals hibernate and they are ready for their sleep
R estful mornings, it's like Heaven in the clouds above the sun
V egetables, scrumptious to eat, go down your throat smoothly
E ating apples, very crunchy, smell lovely
S ilky grass on the ground, a big, big seed, maybe a melon, I don't know
T asty lettuce called an iceberg, amazing to eat.

Chloë Johnston (8)
Astwood Bank First School, Redditch

Harvest

H ear snuffling, spiky hedgehogs searching for big, juicy, wiggly worms.
A nimals searching for food before hibernating.
R ustling leaves on the ground.
V egetables are ripe to pick and store for winter.
E ating all the delicious foods from harvest time.
S ee the conkers falling to the ground.
T wirling, rustling leaves floating to the ground.

Poppy Marshall (8)
Astwood Bank First School, Redditch

Harvest

H edgehogs snuffling for juicy, wiggly worms.
A pples are soft and appley in apple pies.
R abbits, cute, fluffy, little baby rabbits munching on carrots.
V eggies, tasty in gravy.
E ggs, tasty and fresh.
S quirrels hunting for nuts.
T asty toast and Marmite on autumn nights.

Emily Whatmore (9)
Astwood Bank First School, Redditch

Harvest

H ear the whistling of the chilly autumn breeze
A nimals running through the rustling leaves
R ed juicy apples that everyone wants to eat
V egetables waiting to be dug out of the damp ground
E verything is slowing down for the winter sleep
S unset glowing in the evening sky and the lovely moon is smiling
   at me when I go to bed
T asty food to eat at harvest time.

Jessica Grant (8)
Astwood Bank First School, Redditch

Harvest

H ow do tough conkers grow defending themselves from animals.
A pples are all getting munched by spiky hedgehogs before
   they hibernate.
R usty leaves are falling off rattling trees.
V egetables are growing massive for you to eat them.
E very tree is growing tons of lovely crunchy leaves before they fall.
S ilky sunsets making shady seeds grow for food.
T asty nuts are growing massive to eat.

James Goddard (8)
Astwood Bank First School, Redditch

Harvest

H ear the red and orange leaves crunching.
A pples being eaten by squirrels.
R attling trees when the wind is blowing.
V egetables getting harvested by farmers from the enormous fields.
E ating the fresh fruit and vegetables.
S unsets in the evening when there's a red sky.
T asty vegetables fresh from the ground.

Ryan Sellers (8)
Astwood Bank First School, Redditch

Harvest

H ear cute little squirrels chewing the nuts
A nimals running safely from the farmers
R ustling conkers when people accidentally trod on them
V egetables and fruit are so important at this time of year
E very night hedgehogs are outside rattling leaves
S quirrels are rustling leaves like mad
T wirling leaves.

Evie Crane (8)
Astwood Bank First School, Redditch

ONCE UPON a RHYME – The UK

Harvest

H ear the misty breeze blowing against the swaying trees
A pples dropping from the swaying trees
R obins flying through the misty, foggy air
V egetables getting picked for hungry families
E ating lovely, crunchy, crispy carrots
S mell the lovely smell of autumn
T asty, crunchy, crispy carrots.

Matthew Yapp (8)
Astwood Bank First School, Redditch

Harvest

H edgehogs shuffling on the silky grass
A pples crashing to the cold ground
R ich golden leaves on the wet ground
V egetables and meat ready to be eaten
E choing people in the distance
S ticky sap off the trees
T rees twirling in the distance.

Callum Norris (8)
Astwood Bank First School, Redditch

21

Harvest

H appy joys of conkers falling from trees.
A round the big trees is the dewy grass.
R attling, crispy, twirling sounds.
V iews of big oak trees twirling in the sky.
E choing off the big trees, whistling.
S mall pieces of dirt rolling on the ground.
T he nice sight of the sunset.

Ben Green (8)
Astwood Bank First School, Redditch

Mars

His eyes are like fireballs,
Mars is a big ball of burning gas,
If you stepped on it without a spacesuit,
That day would be your last.

His face is fiery red,
He is always very angry,
So you don't want to see him in a mood,
Or he might think you're his food.

Katy Ryan (10)
Charter Primary School, Coventry

The Moon

The moon is a shining ball of light
And shines just for you,
But sometimes keeps its light tight,
And doesn't let it go.

When it shines
Its beautiful face is for everyone to see,
It's a rocky, bumpy planet that looks like it's made of granite.

Ashleigh Hall (10)
Charter Primary School, Coventry

Howler Monkey

H owling all the time.
O nce - never once silent.
W ealthy monkey.
L ike the boss of the army.
E very animal can hear them.
R ainforest animal.

M onkey type.
O rang-utans swinging on branches.
N ever a moment's silence.
K iller plants on the ground.
E very 7-10 miles you can hear them.
Y elling howler monkeys.

Erin Pyper (9)
Clerkhill School, Peterhead

The Rainforest

T rees grow green and tall
H owler monkeys howling loudly
E xotic sites of waterfalls

R aining warm rainforests
A nimals, some big, some small
I think it's beautiful and warm
N oises and sounds
F orest so warm
O rang-utans jumping from tree to tree
R apids pulling animals in
E very animal makes a different noise
S mart animals, silly animals
T hreatened rainforest, will it disappear?

Dion Junor (9)
Clerkhill School, Peterhead

Rainforests

R ains every day in the rainforest.
A lot of noise, animals being silly.
I nsects on the forest floor.
N oisy on every single layer.
F orest floor is very wet.
O rang-utans are in the canopy layer.
R are animals in every layer.
E ggs on the forest floor.
S outh America the Amazon is in.
T allest trees in the world.

Aidan Low (8)
Clerkhill School, Peterhead

Rainforest

Come to the rainforest, you'll see tall trees,
Waterfalls and leaves flutter by.
You'll hear howling monkeys, leaves rustling and water dripping.
The rainforest is a beautiful, wonderful, lovely, pretty
And a colourful place.
So come and see the rainforest,
You'll feel very happy.

Cara MacIntosh (9)
Clerkhill School, Peterhead

The Rainforest

In the rainforest there is such a good sight.
Some shall dazzle your eyes.
Exotic sights you have never seen.
It shall dazzle your eyes like nothing you know.

Twigs break but was it me?
Then a tree fell down and there was a thump!
The animals were screaming and shouting,
What could it be?
It sounded loud but I could still hear the birds,
Then that calmed me down.

I felt happy and a little scared because it was a bit creepy,
But I was OK.
The thing that scared me was that I was all alone.

Lee Stephen (9)
Clerkhill School, Peterhead

Rainforest

R ainforests always get rain
A nimals moving everywhere
I n the rainforest, hundreds of animals around
N o rainforests in 2030
F ind the three rainforest tribes
O rang-utans stay in the canopy
R ainforests get cut down every day
E very product from the rainforest, mostly have a sign
S top people cutting down trees.
T here are trees all over the forest.

Sophie Sim (9)
Clerkhill School, Peterhead

The Rainforest

T rees
H ome to animals and tribes
E verywhere you go you will hear noise

R ain
A nimals
I t's being chopped down
N ear the equator
F ull of living
O thers still waiting to be discovered
R are animals live there
E ven people live there
S loths are one of the animals that live there
T here are waterfalls.

Alison Young (9)
Clerkhill School, Peterhead

This Is The Rainforest

Come to the rainforest it has exotic lives and exotic sights.
You will see the lives of the sweet animals that drift by the water life.
All the gentle drifting feelings will just blow you away
to a waterfall sight.
It has the hot and steaming water flowing by.
All you can hear is a little smooth water everywhere.
You can hear the wind blowing through the air.
The animals will creep up slowly and dazzle your eyes.
They are bright and sweet but hardly anything you can hear.
The sweet bright flowers are colourful too.
Just come to the rainforest, it is the only place with colour in it.

Lauren Davidson (9)
Clerkhill School, Peterhead

The Rainforest

The toucan is big.
The toucan has a big bill.
The toucan is a poor flier.
The toucan sounds loud.
The toucan is slow.
The toucan is colourful.
The toucan is cool.
I like the toucan.

Lauren Milne (9)
Clerkhill School, Peterhead

Pandas

Pandas looking all around for food.
Big pandas, small pandas all around.
Cute, funny little babies crunching on bamboo.
Moving on all four legs.
Such a beautiful sight to see.

Shannon Craighead (9)
Clerkhill School, Peterhead

The Rainforest

It rains so much it cannot stop.
The rain patters on the leaves,
It patters on my head and patters on the floor
Until it goes to its bed.
The plants grow up, up, up until they stop.
I can see the bird flying above me
And the howler monkeys howling so loud
I can't hear myself think.
I am boiling like an oven.
I am excited
Until everyone and everything goes *quiet!*

Gemma Mackie (9)
Clerkhill School, Peterhead

Rainforest

R ain is dropping from the leaves in the rainforest.
A mazing sights in the rainforest.
I t's sunny for two hours in the rainforest.
N ature is everywhere in the rainforest.
F ruit is on the trees in the rainforest.
O rang-utans swing from tree to tree in the rainforest.
R ed eye tree frogs hopping from leaf to leaf in the rainforest.
E lephants charging at the trees in the rainforest.
S uch a beautiful sight is the rainforest.
T ry to save the rainforest!

Kirsty Morrison (9)
Clerkhill School, Peterhead

Rainforest

R aging with colour
A beautiful habitat
I love it
N ever new
F ragranced forest
O ld yes
R ainy like mad
E verything lovely
S o hot
T rickling water.

Matthew Lemon (9)
Clerkhill School, Peterhead

Rainforest

R aindrops dripping from the sky.
A ll that I can see are thick trees in the air.
I n the rainforest you're not alone.
N ature is everywhere, where you go in the rainforest.
F orest floor is very dark during day.
O rang-utans swinging tree to tree.
R ed eye tree frogs jumping leaf to leaf.
E verlasting water from waterfalls.
S mooth, cool breezes from the rainforest.
T arantulas getting their prey.

Ryan Ritchie (9)
Clerkhill School, Peterhead

Rainforest

R ainforests are colourful and dark.
A mazing sight is the Amazon.
I nstead of lying on the ground go to the rainforest.
N ature is the best.
F orests are nothing like rainforests.
O rang-utans make big nests.
R ainforests are the best.
E mergent layer is the top of a tree.
S ome people live in the rainforest.
T he rain travels from branch to branch.

Aaron Buchan (9)
Clerkhill School, Peterhead

Chameleons

C urling up tail.
H abitat is great.
A n insect eater.
M ostly camouflaged.
E xplores the rainforest.
L ong sticky tongue.
E xciting animals.
O n sight of its prey.
N ever gets lost.
S ly animal.

Talia Davidson (9)
Clerkhill School, Peterhead

Sloths

S low as a snail.
L oudly upside down on a branch.
O n trees, high up in the sky.
T all sloths.
H airy as a lion's beard.
S mall as a stick insect.

Jay Dyson (9)
Clerkhill School, Peterhead

Howler Monkeys

H owler monkeys are very loud.
O ur monkeys are in Edinburgh zoo.
W ondering if howler monkeys are happy animals.
L emons howler monkeys don't like.
E very day howler monkeys scream.
R unning monkeys like best.

M onkeys are funny and they eat bananas.
O ur monkey howls are not loud.
N ot our favourite monkeys.
K ind and generous our monkeys are.
E very day howler monkeys show.
Y ikes, watch out that they don't get you.
S houts, noisy animals they are.

Jenna Warrender (9)
Clerkhill School, Peterhead

The Rainforest

R ustling leaves on the forest floor
A mphibians like frogs go hopping along
I guanas, snakes and other reptiles
N atural plants twisting and tangling
F alling branches and broken twigs
O rang-utans, gorillas and many more
R ocks and rubble fall with the flow of the waterfalls
E nchanting sights of greenery
S weat and mist gathers around me
T earing apart it shall not be!

Abby Grant (9)
Clerkhill School, Peterhead

The Rainforest

R ainy all the time
A ctive animals in the rainforest
I nteresting sounds to hear
N ow in danger as we speak
F ighting the battle to save the rainforest
O rang-utans to see
R iver running through the rainforest
E nding as time goes by
S aving it is the answer
T ry it and feel good, save the rainforest.

Morgan Cruickshank (9)
Clerkhill School, Peterhead

Rocket Ear Piercing

Summer has died,
Autumn's attacked.
He murders vegetables and makes them pay,
then the rest just run away!
He rips the leaves from their trees.

Autumn wears a rocket ear piercing,
he adorns himself with his dirty brown leaf coat.
His shoes are made from a bare bark chestnut tree.
Winter comes along
and then throws her glistening snowballs at his head.
Autumn tumbles down in pain.

Lennon Bailey (10)
Conisbrough Balby Street Primary School, Doncaster

Ruby Red Fury

Autumn has killed Summer and has taken over the land!
The leaves fall to the ground in surrender.
He makes the vegetables shoot out of their homes in fear.
A wave of his wooden sword
makes the leaves turn aged and crinkled.

He wears a crisp red leaf suit.
Autumn has furry bear skin shoes that are covered in blood.
His eyes light up with ruby red fury.
His hat is made from fox skins,
with the tails dangling as tassels.

Morgan Winstanley (10)
Conisbrough Balby Street Primary School, Doncaster

Swoosh!

Summer has outstayed her welcome,
Autumn shakes his golden head in despair.
He yanks the petite plants from the green grass
and stomps on their roots in rage.

Swoosh! The trees dance in the breeze
as the wind whistles in fear.
Autumn burns the leaves as he cries,
everything goes silent as everything dies . . .

Autumn is wearing a leaf jacket
burnt by the matches and flames.
Around his neck is a bronze tie
with a Catherine wheel lit up with sparks of fire.
Autumn adorns himself with pig-sty soil trouser bottoms.

Shannon Meggitt (10)
Conisbrough Balby Street Primary School, Doncaster

The Autumn Man

Autumn shoves Summer out of the land and takes over.
He shakes the trees until the leaves fall off.
He kicks the vegetables until they scream out of their homes into the basket.

Autumn wears a white misty shirt,
with a leafy red and gold tie that stands out wherever he goes.
He wears soil shorts that feel horrible,
and on his feet he has shoes made from bugs.

Beth Wright (10)
Conisbrough Balby Street Primary School, Doncaster

Autumn Has Invaded

Autumn killed Summer as he invaded!
He fiercely burnt the leaves off the trees.
Autumn ripped the vegetables from their roots.
They cried because they had lost their wriggly toes.
Autumn pulled the grass up
and turned it into black and brown soil.
The vegetables limped and then collapsed
into their underground homes.

Autumn was wearing bright orange pumpkin shoes
with roots for laces.
He made a massive hole in a conker and wore it as a ring.
Autumn wore a black top hat
with firework sparklers on top that shone at midnight.
He collected all the grain from the bare fields
and kept it in his pockets because he liked to steal things.
Autumn showed off his snazzy strawberry gold chains,
and made a plan to battle against Winter.

Bradley Phillips (10)
Conisbrough Balby Street Primary School, Doncaster

Autumn Has Raided

Summer has surrendered during Autumn's raid.
Autumn drags himself across the golden fields in rage.
He burns the leaves to a crisp
and tears the emerald leaves off the shivering trees.
A fierce explosion of his rocket,
makes the vegetables abandon their homes in fear.

Autumn wears a burnt black shirt,
which makes everything bare and brown when he passes.
His eyes are like fire; a dark crimson colour.
Autumn has a hat made from old cobweb silk,
it's infested with garden spiders.
His shoes are made from leaves,
which have surrendered to Autumn's evilness.
In his pocket he has his rocket,
that makes everything fear him.
Will Autumn ever be defeated?

Reece Groves (10)
Conisbrough Balby Street Primary School, Doncaster

Clip-Clop

Autumn is back again to take over!
He grabs the green leaves and turns them orange.
Then he swoops down swiftly, scooping up vegetables.
He has got flames upon his head that crackle like a bonfire.

Autumn is wearing a jacket made from the bark of a tree.
He has got shoes made out of wood that clip-clop as he walks.
He wears trousers made from grass that have worms wriggling in them.

Ethan Hughes (10)
Conisbrough Balby Street Primary School, Doncaster

Autumn Man

Summer has gone on holiday
and autumn has come to stay.
He is picking apples
as he swiftly strolls across the land,
kicking the colourful leaves.
Autumn jumps on the clouds
making the air misty and dull.
Autumn is wearing a cobweb top,
that has a Catherine wheel that spins around.
Upon his head is a twig hat.
He yanks the vegetables out of the dull ground.

Millie Cole (10)
Conisbrough Balby Street Primary School, Doncaster

Autumn Finally Appears

In a flash of light Autumn finally appears.
He plucks the timid stained leaves off the trees.
All the leaves have a makeover.
The Autumn Man wears a smoky suit of flaky bark.
He also wears shoes that are as grey as dried up soil.
He wears the finest, lush golden leaves on his hat.
In his eyes shines the flame of Bonfire Night.
Autumn wears the abandoned summer tomatoes round his neck.
He wears a Catherine wheel as a bow tie,
While he plans a surprise party for Winter.

Kian Dearden (10)
Conisbrough Balby Street Primary School, Doncaster

Stepping Out Of The Shadows

Autumn steps out of the shadows,
and sends a gush of wind that makes the leaves shiver.
He kidnaps the vegetables
and stores them away in the darkness.
He tears the leaves from branches
and abandons them to flutter to the ground.
Autumn screams a crack of thunder,
and sneezes a flash of light.
Autumn wears a lush root suit;
the revolting roots dangle from his shoulders
with slugs sauntering up his arms.
His trousers overlap with orange crispy leaves,
and his hat is fashioned from cobwebs
with spiders dangling from the webs.
Autumn's shoes are formed of mud
moulded into shape by his filthy hands.
As it turns to the end of Autumn's time,
the day fades and mist overlaps the country.
He strides back into the shadows
and waits for the next year to come.

Emily Hancock (10)
Conisbrough Balby Street Primary School, Doncaster

Cobweb Coat

Autumn stomps his way into the new season.
He crashes into the trees and tears the leaves down
throwing them on the ground.
As the leaves come crashing down
Autumn rips the lovely vegetables from their grubby homes.

Autumn is wearing firework trousers
with brown twig shoes.
Autumn has hair made from spiky thorns
and he always wears a cobweb coat.

Bradie Wordsworth (10)
Conisbrough Balby Street Primary School, Doncaster

Autumn Battles

With one final swipe,
Summer plummets to the dungeon of things past.
Autumn orders the leaves to bow down to him,
or it means war!
He commands the vegetables to leave their homes
before torture is required.
He's polite to the sun,
and gives him a warm, cloudy coat.

He wears a carved out pumpkin lid helmet
and gold battle armour.
He always keeps his orange leafy sword at hand.
Autumn also wears a pair of crimson twig sandals
made with the finest oak in the forest.

Matthew Hancock (10)
Conisbrough Balby Street Primary School, Doncaster

Rocket Trousers

Summer has died, but Autumn is born.
He gently brushes the trees with his rake
that has bronze and gold dye at the end.
With one swipe all the leaves are bronze and gold
with the trees bare and brown.
The vegetables come with laughter
while he sends them to his friends.

Autumn wears a suit
that has leaves attached that plummet,
but they stick and more come down
like it's being projected.
He also wears a rocket top as a hat
while the body of the rockets are his trousers
with a daisy chain from Summer.

James Ellor (10)
Conisbrough Balby Street Primary School, Doncaster

The Mountains

M ountain, the high point in the valley.
O ut on the mountain the trees rustle in the wind.
U p in the misty sky the birds sing happily.
N ice views wherever you look.
T rees surround you up the peaceful mountain.
A round you the nice sound of the wind.
I n the valleys surrounded by mountains.
N o noise, no people, no traffic.

Jordon Barrett (10)
Cwmclydach Primary School, Tonypandy

Chocolate

C hocolate is a favourite gift for children.
H omes and places, children love chocolate.
O n the train, also bus.
C hocolate is a scrummy bar.
O h please,' the children say.
L ater no nagging and begging.
A lright,' parents say day and night.
T uesday is a good day to have chocolate.
E ight o'clock; I have a hot chocolate.

Cody Homer (10)
Cwmclydach Primary School, Tonypandy

Ice Cream

I 'm sitting on the beach eating ice cream
C old as ice but I'm enjoying it
E veryone loves ice cream in the hot weather

C an I have another ice cream please?' I say to the van
R elaxing on the beach with my chocolate ice cream
E ating my ice cream, everyone notices how nice it is
A nyone want another ice cream?' I say
M *mm,* lovely and cold.

Cerys Baker (10)
Cwmclydach Primary School, Tonypandy

Friends

A friend is a friend
Who's there for each other
Who cares and helps
And bothers with each

I watched the sun gleaming
And then we started screaming
And then we started sunbathing

We sang on the grass
And then we saw a class
We laughed and played
And there we stayed.

Rhian Hayward (10)
Cwmclydach Primary School, Tonypandy

The Way Through A Football Game

The supporters gathering round to see the game.
The players running onto the pitch.
The referee blows the whistle for the game to start.
The crowd are singing really loud.
One of the teams scores.
The crowd are going wild,
Shouting, 'Come on!'

The field is really muddy.
The players get really muddy.
The referee blows the whistle for half-time.
The players have a break to get their drinks.

The players come running back on.
The whistle blows for the second half.
The other team scores.
The crowd are really loud.
There are four minutes' stoppage time.
One of the teams scores again.
The crowd are shouting, 'Come on' and 'well done.'
The whistle goes, the game finishes.
Success for our team!

Cameron Clarke (10)
Cwmclydach Primary School, Tonypandy

The Volcano Poem

The deadly volcano blows its top
The lava runs out like a coffee pot
It's sticky, it's hot
It will boil your bot
So stay away or you will get hot.

Jordan Cammish (10)
Edith Moorhouse Primary School, Carterton

The Friendship

A friend to me is like a star in the sky.
Someone who will always listen to me
And be there when I cry,
Talk to me because I am me
And talk to me because you like me.
Let us always hang out
And look out for each other,
Visit the shops
And buy lots of goodies,
But always remember
Not to be bullies.

Carla Watts (10)
Edith Moorhouse Primary School, Carterton

Christmas

Christmas is in December, the last month of the year
It snows all the time
The snow hugs the top of the houses
Children receiving presents and reindeer in the park
Falling night sky
Choirs singing to families as they knock on the doors
Sleigh bells from Santa's sleigh
Christmas trees are up in everyone's houses
Christmas is exciting
Children waiting to hear Santa come down the chimney
Christmas comes only once a year.

Reece Fennel (10)
Edith Moorhouse Primary School, Carterton

Friends And Family

The endless spill of excitement and fun,
Got family and friends dancing around the sparkling sun.

Paddling pool with a slippery slide,
Under the water we go to hide.
Children shouting, 'Here we come,'
To play and have lots of fun.

Sizzling sausages, burgers and cheese,
The lucky one cooking shouted, 'Hurry up or I'll eat all of these.'

Families are special and so are our friends,
Special memories we hold will never come to an end.

Shona Manning (10)
Edith Moorhouse Primary School, Carterton

Daisy, My Dog

Daisy is a teddy bear up close for a hug.
Daisy is a model walking proudly in her coat.
Daisy has her pink bandana wrapped around her shoulders.
Daisy is the horse trotting round the garden.
Daisy has the playfulness of a child in a playground.
Daisy has the love of 10 million beating hearts.
That's why Daisy is the best Jack Russell dog for me.

Emily Bird (10)
Edith Moorhouse Primary School, Carterton

Fishing

F ishing is fun
I n the winter or the sun.
S itting in my chair
H oping the carp are there.
I n it comes, it's a double
N ever gone through so much trouble.
G otcha!

Danny Allsworth (10)
Edith Moorhouse Primary School, Carterton

Favourite Pets

I have a dog called Holly,
She is very, very jolly.
She likes her walks
But cannot talk.
She likes to lick
And catch a stick.
She's chocolate brown
And likes to roll around.
She'll do a trick for a treat.
She loves her cuddles
But now stepping in puddles.

We do lots together
And I'll love her forever.

Ellen Chadwick (10)
Edith Moorhouse Primary School, Carterton

Charlie Miller

Charlie is mad as a Mexican's dog always jumping around.
He's like a forest fire that never stops burning.
Charlie is a chocoholic in a sweet factory
Always bursting with excitement.
He is like a newspaper press cutting the words out.
Charlie is a bonfire sparkling with ideas.
He is a comedian, always putting a wide grin across your face
And that's my friend, Charlie.

Cameron Bilton (10)
Edith Moorhouse Primary School, Carterton

In The Dark Night

It was cold and wet,
Dark and gloomy,
Still and silent,
An ice-cold tickle ran down my spine,
A shiver grew inside me.

Standing and staring,
Not knowing what to do.
Behind me a figure dashed,
I turned . . . nothing.

Then the sound of rustling leaves
I turned . . . still nothing.

I started to feel scared.
A dark shadow hovered in the sky,
Now I was really scared,
Another dark shadow appeared out of nowhere.

A huge cold hand clamped tightly around my mouth,
Now I was terrified.
Would I ever see daylight again . . . ?

Ella Standdon (10)
Edith Moorhouse Primary School, Carterton

Rugby

Rugby is like a ball flying through mid-air like a jet plane,
It's pushing and shoving, trying to get the ball.
It's the players' charging down the field, hoping to score a try.
Rugby is mud flying into your face as players tackle you into the ground.
It's the thrill of taking a penalty kick
And watching the ball fly through the tower-like posts.
The match is over and the pain is worth the win.

Joe Delaney (10)
Edith Moorhouse Primary School, Carterton

One Of A Kind

My pet Billy is one of a kind
There's no one else like him.
He's a flickering light bulb in the silent darkness.

A breath of fresh air.
He's a beating heart, begging for love.
A ball of fluff, so simple yet so fun.
He's chewing gum, never losing his taste.

My pet Billy is one of a kind,
There's no one else like him.

He's a bottle of Coke fizzing with energy,
As energetic as a bouncy ball.
A lightning bolt soaring across the skies
As light as rays of sun in your eyes.

My pet Billy is one of a kind,
There's no one else like him.

George Meyer (10)
Edith Moorhouse Primary School, Carterton

Rosie

My rabbit Rosie,
Loves to play,
Hopping around the garden,
In her own little way.
With her sister Sandy,
She loves to dig,
Scratching and crawling,
Ooh what a trick.
Rosie is a lazy bunny,
She lies down on happy feet,
And lets the sun tickle her tummy,
Until it's time for her to eat.
For all these things,
I love her so,
She is perfect to me,
So let it show . . .

Lucy Goodwin (10)
Edith Moorhouse Primary School, Carterton

Grandma

My grandma isn't that old,
She's got her own teeth and she's not going bald,
She walks with a stick but that doesn't matter,
Because I love her anyway, she's as mad as a hatter,
She lives on her own in her very small home,
With her two little dogs that sit on her knee,
Lick her face and drink all her tea,
She loves her two dogs, they give her so much fun,
She likes to take them out and give them a good run,
I love my grandma, she makes me laugh,
She washes my hair, she gives me a bath,
She scrubs my neck, she makes it red raw,
Take a good look it really is sore,
So if you see my grandma walking through town,
Give her a wave, you'll see her around.

Georgia Boyd (10)
Edith Moorhouse Primary School, Carterton

About Mr Jones

Mr Jones is like a football,
Always bouncing around with joy.

Mr Jones is like a bomb,
Ready to explode when there's too much racket.

He is like a pen with never-ending ink,
Always flowing with ideas.

Like a calculator always adding up sums,
Never knows when to stop.

Mr Jones is like sticky glue,
Always gets stuck in there.

That's Mr Jones for you.

Bayley Dynan (10)
Edith Moorhouse Primary School, Carterton

My Family

Family to me is love and understanding
A support like a cushion to make a safe landing.

We sometimes argue, we sometimes fight,
But we always have a cuddle by the end of the night.

Happiness and having fun
Is playing games with Dad and Mum.

Mum and Dad and me make three,
The happy Newman family.

Gareth Newman (10)
Edith Moorhouse Primary School, Carterton

My Dog

I once had a dog called Ted
He slept at the end of my bed
He'd snore and snore
Until he fell on the floor
That's why he now sleeps in the shed.

Martin Rhodes (10)
Edith Moorhouse Primary School, Carterton

When Saturday Comes

I wake up early at the crack of dawn
Pull back my curtains, no time to yawn.
I'm excited and nervous about the day,
In a few hours' time, our first game we will play.

Grab my shin pads and boots, throw them in my bag,
Nothing else matters, I'm footy mad.
My mum shouts, 'Oi, you forgot your drink!'
So I jog back to her with a smile and a wink.
My feet hardly touch the ground as I sprint to the car
First home game today, so not that far.

I think of myself walking out at Old Trafford to trumpets and drums.
This always happens . . . when Saturday comes.

Travis Cozier (10)
Edith Moorhouse Primary School, Carterton

Football Match

Footballs here, footballs there,
Parents yelling everywhere,
Managers stressing all the time,
Referee running up and down,
Linesmen waving their flags left and right,
Decisions right or wrong,
Now it's finished let's move on,
Final whistle, final kick,
Get in the car and zoom home quick.

Mehmet Sekmen (10)
Edith Moorhouse Primary School, Carterton

Jonah

Jonah has a cold, wet nose,
Velvety, floppy ears and sharp, scratchy toes.
He jumps, he barks, his tail wags
And when we take him out we take poo bags.
He chews the carrots and Mum's old shoe
And follows you around, even to the loo.
Jonah is the sunshine in my life,
Making me happy every day.
Jonah is a Hoover, cleaning up the floor.

Sasha Harley (10)
Edith Moorhouse Primary School, Carterton

The Park Bench

Spring is beautiful as birds tweet in the trees.
The smell of freshly-mown grass fills the air.
Spiderwebs glisten on me.
Ducks being fed from people sitting on me
And a fresh lick of paint is brushed upon me.

Summer brings sunflowers and marigolds.
I can hear children playing happily.
Apples red and juicy-looking.
The trees a luxurious green colour.

Autumn is when the trees go golden
And there are conkers all over the leaf-covered ground.
The smell of bonfires fills the air.
I feel the rain splatter down on me.

Winter is the time when the snow falls,
Which makes icicles form on me.
I can see snowmen being made by children
And the sky gets dark at 5pm.

I sit here waiting patiently for what will happen next?

Jodie Aikman (10)
Edith Moorhouse Primary School, Carterton

Cheetahs

I am Shadow, I'm the king of all cheetahs,
And I'm also the world's fastest cheetah.
I can run up to seventy miles per hour at full pace.
I'm the strongest ever.

But of course there has to be a rival,
His name is Simba, he's the king of all the lions around the world.
He's more powerful and stronger,
But I'm faster and cleverer than him.
A magical spirit once told me that he's coming for me
So I'm ready for him every single day.
He's travelling all the way from Kenya, I'm in Zimbabwe.

It's been eleven years since the spirit came to me
And I think the battle is about to begin.
Suddenly I hear a mighty and fierce roar.
Then I turn around. In the distance,
'I see him,' I say to everyone near.
And he's not alone.
He's got all of his lion male fighters.
I call my fighters together.
Both lion fighters and cheetah fighters charge at each other.
They both slash into each other,
Ripping each other's flesh and bones out.

Kingsley Cummings (10)
Edith Moorhouse Primary School, Carterton

The Potion

In the potion went . . .
An eye of newt
Wart of frog
A smelly boot
A hair of hog
Some fingernails freshly cut
This gruesome potion never fails
But don't forget the golfing putt
The fuzz stuck in your PC's mouse
A dirty sock from round the house
Alien gloop, fish tank poop
Makes the base of a really good soup
TV dust that sits and waits
And some dirty dinner plates
All these Mum should have done
She went and put them all in one
I really am quite amused
At how my mum gets so confused
She was meant to be cleaning up you see
But instead we're having Mum's potion for tea.

Kate Williams (10)
Edith Moorhouse Primary School, Carterton

Chocolate

Chocolate, chocolate, chocolate,
The taste of luxurious melting chocolate in your mouth.
Chocolate, chocolate, chocolate,
The softness of chocolate rubbing softly on your gum.
Chocolate, chocolate, chocolate,
My mind is crazy about chocolate.
Chocolate, chocolate, chocolate
And finally home with my bar of chocolate on the sofa.

Charlotte Smart (10)
Edith Moorhouse Primary School, Carterton

Monster Trucks

When the monster trucks started up they were like thunder.
All of them went around the stadium like a hurricane of giant metal trucks.
Smashing small cars to smithereens as they jumped the car stacks.
One after another they tried to do the biggest jump
As each truck came closer to me
And did its jump over the car stack.
When they landed it felt like an earthquake
And my heart beat faster with excitement.
It was a good job I had the ear plugs.
I felt sorry for Monster Mutt.
She landed on her roof then on her side,
So she could escape from her roof hatch.
She looked a little shaken but OK.
All in all I had the perfect day.

Elliot Langstaff (9)
Edith Moorhouse Primary School, Carterton

Football

Me and my dad, we both love football
But the games are different as can be.

In his he supports the Packers, they wear cheese on their heads!
I support United and call it soccer instead.

We are both very passionate supporters.
My game is played in two halves.
In his they pick up and run with the ball
And his game is played in four quarters.

The games are very different but have much in common too.
We both score goals, have referees and both make substitutes.

The time we spend together is the best time of all,
Having fun together
Watching the game we call football.

James Turvey (9)
Edith Moorhouse Primary School, Carterton

Train Journey

I'm going on a journey very far
I'm going by train and by car
When we go past the sheep
The train goes *chug, chug, beep*
Inside the carriage I'm playing with my toys
Outside the carriage there is lots of noise
Clackety clack, clackety clack
That's the sound of the train on the track
Now the journey's coming to the end
On the platform I see my friend.

Anna Simmonds (9)
Edith Moorhouse Primary School, Carterton

My Family

My mum is as nice as chocolate cake,
When I am upset my mum always makes me feel better.
My mum does a lot of things for me
Like taking me to my football matches.
My mum always gets me great presents for my birthday and Christmas.

My dad is as nice as ice cream with strawberry sauce and sprinkles.
My dad is the person who talked me into playing for a football team
And now I really enjoy it.
My dad took me to see my first ever football match at Swindon.
My dad always plays football with me in the garden
And he makes up fun games.

My brother always lets me play on his computer games
Like 'Super Mario Bros'.
My brother always plays games with me in the house and in the garden.
The only thing that is bad about my brother is that he is always annoying me.

Jack Bellenger (9)
Edith Moorhouse Primary School, Carterton

Autumn

Autumn days when the rain's falling,
Shining brightly in the sun.
Coldness beaten by the smell of bacon,
Sudden rain showers make me run.

Crunch of leaves as I walk to school,
Golden, brown and yellow they drift.
Breaking quietly when they fall to the ground,
Woodland walks are so much fun.

Samuel Williams (9)
Edith Moorhouse Primary School, Carterton

Rabbit Elizabeth

One of my best friends, Elizabeth,
A rabbit,
She is soft, cuddly and warm
And she is always up for a little cuddle.

She isn't just a pet to me,
She's family too
And family matters,
So my little friend loves me.

This is nearing the end of my little poem,
Just like Elizabeth
Because she is short,
She even has a best friend called Biscuit.
And forever we are together.

Lucy Collett (9)
Edith Moorhouse Primary School, Carterton

Stars

High up in the silky blue sky
Where rainbows sing and birds fly
Silver and bright shine in the night
At dark they are here and in the day they disappear
Thousands of miles from Earth
Fire and rock gave them birth
Millions and millions of stars all together
Have been hanging around the Earth forever
Bigger than ten of the sun
That's massive plus immense - it must be for fun!
Small ones, big ones, green, pink and blue
There in the sky just for you . . .
Oh and you get stars in your eyes
What a surprise!

Molly Smith (9)
Edith Moorhouse Primary School, Carterton

My Cat Tilly

My cat Tilly is black as the night
She creeps up behind me and gives me a fright
Her eyes are bright yellow and shine like the stars
She wades through the grass but runs from the cars
Curled on my bed she snuggles in tight
My cat Tilly, black as the night.

Hollie Walton (10)
Edith Moorhouse Primary School, Carterton

Meadow

Long tall grass,
Winds are blowing,
Fluffy white clouds in light blue sky.
Blackberries, bright black, ripe and ready to be picked,
Flashing red ladybirds crawling over leaves.
The sound of flowing water from the stream,
The meadow is here.

Conor Wright (9)
Edith Moorhouse Primary School, Carterton

Scarecrow

If I was a scarecrow,
I'd scare those birds away.

If I was a scarecrow,
I'd stand in a field all day.

If I was a scarecrow,
I'd have creepy crawlies living in me.

If I was a scarecrow,
Night would be creepy and scary.

If I was a scarecrow
The sun would be like a fireball
Melting and breaking into pieces down on me.

It would make me feel glowy, gleamy and sloppy
But very happy.

Tommy Matthews (9)
Edith Moorhouse Primary School, Carterton

My Dog

My dog speaks to me when he wants his food,
He also shouts when he's in a mood,
My dog walks in circles when he needs a poo,
He also gets angry when I tell him, 'Shoo.'
When my dog jumps he means play,
He usually always gets his way,
My dog can do everything I say,
Especially when I say, 'Let's play.'

Grace Ford (9)
Edith Moorhouse Primary School, Carterton

A Broken Teddy Bear

My eye slowly falling out like a tear falling off my cheek.
My auto sound slowly running out of batteries
Like my sore throat slowly losing my voice.
Sitting by the cold pink wall,
I need a soft warm bed to sleep for eleven hours.
Being picked up, cuddled like a loved baby.
I am now old, tatty and falling apart.
It might be time for me to go into the dark cold . . . *bin!*

Bethany Summerfield (11)
Edith Moorhouse Primary School, Carterton

The Fence

We made a fence, it's seven foot tall.
It stretches like the great China wall.
It's made from big posts of wood
Dug in the ground as tall as I stood.
It's chocolate brown and held up with nails,
The strength of this fence it never fails.

Brendan Sayer (9)
Edith Moorhouse Primary School, Carterton

The Beach

The sound of the waves on the pebbles as I wake up,
Birds flying in the sky trying to catch their early morning fish,
Children giggling as they touch the sand,
Buckets and spades are ready to make the biggest sandcastles,
I jump over the waves as the water goes to the shore,
Halfway through and I enjoy an ice cream,
Time to explore the rock pools, 'Hello Mr Crab,'
Fish swimming around my feet as I paddle in the sea,
I need a rest and read my book under my umbrella
Blowing slightly in the wind,
The day at the beach is over and the sea is calm,
Children are tired, time to go home,
The sound of the waves on the pebbles as I fall asleep.

Ellen Cole (9)
Edith Moorhouse Primary School, Carterton

Puppy

P uppies always on the move
U p and down they jump
P laying all day chasing their tails
P eace and quiet when they cuddle up and go to sleep
Y apping and barking till the sun goes down.

Daniel Webb (9)
Edith Moorhouse Primary School, Carterton

Football

F ans in the stands
O utstanding goal
O ffside flag is up again
T eams in the changing room, it's half-time
B alls in the back of the net
A way fans demanding a penalty
L osing team disappointed
L eague title won.

Jack Barber (10)
Edith Moorhouse Primary School, Carterton

The Wind

The wind is a hairdryer,
A hairdryer of coldness.
The wind is a screamer,
A screamer of whistles.
The wind is a shaker,
A shaker of the trees
But most of all the wind is the wind.

Harry Brown (9)
Edith Moorhouse Primary School, Carterton

Fishing

The rising sun as it shines on the glimmering water
The running water rolling over the riverbed
Wind rushing through the dancing reeds
The diving kingfisher catching fish
The wild geese guard their babies as they clap their beaks in search of food
Pestering swans sneaking your bait
Grey herons stand like statues waiting to dart a fish
The sound of a songthrush singing to his mate
Water voles scurrying through the grass
Colourful dragonfly hovering over the water
Mosquitoes buzzing in your ear
Patrolling fish breaking the surface as they suntan in the morning light
Shimmering fish as they shoot away from the predator's perch
Bursting bubbles of the fish feeding off the ground
And all this is broken by the screaming reel
As a carp tears through the lily pads.

Ryan Campbell (10)
Edith Moorhouse Primary School, Carterton

Clumsy Penguins

Ten quiet penguins standing in a line,
One fell over and pushed the rest, then there were nine.

Nine bored penguins all came out to skate,
One tripped and fell over the gate, then there were eight.

Eight happy penguins playing along with Kevin,
One slipped and broke his leg, then there were seven.

Seven excited penguins warming up their chicks,
One fainted in excitement, then there were six.

Six funny penguins going for a drive,
One went around the bend, then there were five.

Five sad penguins opening the door,
One stepped out and slipped over, then there were four.

Four annoyed penguins washing Lee,
One got knocked over, then there were three.

Three stroppy penguins tying their shoes,
One tripped over their laces, then there were two.

Two tired penguins calling for their mum,
One fell asleep, then there was one.

One fed-up penguin waiting for some fun,
He saw a funfair, then there was none.

Briony Clark & Jodie Bell (9)
Gooderstone CE (VA) Primary School, King's Lynn

64

Penguins Go To The Fair

Ten excited penguins all in a line,
One fell off the roller coaster, then there were nine.

Nine excited penguins waiting to skate,
One twisted his ankle, then there were eight.

Eight excited penguins having fun in Devon,
One ate all of the hot dogs, then there were seven.

Seven excited penguins eating a Twix,
One fell asleep, then there were six.

Six excited penguins taking a dive,
One flew off the helter-skelter, then there were five.

Five excited penguins hurry through the door,
One got lost in the fun house, then there were four.

Four excited penguins clamber into a tree,
One got stuck, then there were three.

Three excited penguins waiting for a tattoo,
One got infected, then there were two.

Two excited penguins all having fun,
One found a girlfriend, then there was one.

One excited penguin went back where it begun,
Got on the bus then there were none.

Robert Jestico & Josh Hayhoe (9)
Gooderstone CE (VA) Primary School, King's Lynn

Counting Penguins

Ten tired penguins standing in a line,
One fell down when the fish ran out, then there were nine.

Nine tired penguins worried about their weight,
One ran away on a jog, then there were eight.

Eight tired penguins fishing with Kevin,
One got swallowed by a whale then there were seven.

Seven lazy penguins munching on a Twix,
One went off to watch telly then there were six.

Six tired penguins sliding on a beehive,
One got stung then there were five.

Five lazy penguins eating an apple core,
One choked then there were four.

Four clumsy penguins climbing up a tree,
One slipped and broke his leg, then there were three.

Three sad penguins crying, 'Boo-hoo,'
One ran to Mummy, and then there were two.

Two little penguins, one had an extra long tongue,
One ran to the doctor's, then there was one.

One relaxed penguin sitting in the sun,
One got badly burnt then there were none.

Samuel Gilbert (9) & Kieran D'Aeth (10)
Gooderstone CE (VA) Primary School, King's Lynn

Two Times Table

Two ones are two,
Penguins use shampoo.

Two twos are four,
Penguins on the red see-saw.

Two threes are six,
Naughty penguins up to tricks.

Two fours are eight,
Brainy penguins calculate.

Two fives are ten,
The penguins make a den.

Two sixes are twelve,
Penguins search and delve.

Two sevens are fourteen,
Penguins have a magical dream.

Two eights are sixteen,
Penguins play on the trampoline.

Two nines are eighteen,
Penguins hate to be clean.

Two tens are twenty,
Penguins eat plenty.

Jessica Scrivener (9) & Hannah Gamble (10)
Gooderstone CE (VA) Primary School, King's Lynn

Ten Adventurous Penguins

Ten happy penguins swimming so fine,
One went off to catch a fish then there were nine.

Nine chunky penguins, hate to be late,
One felt faint then there were eight.

Eight merry penguins setting off to Devon,
One took the wrong road then there were seven.

Seven silly penguins feeding the chicks,
One got pecked then there were six.

Six brave penguins dancing around a hive,
One got stung then there were five.

Five adventurous penguins went on a world tour,
One slid off a camel then there were four.

Four clumsy penguins climbed up a tree,
One got stuck then there were three.

Three busy penguins making a stew,
One fell head first into the pot, then there were two.

Two lazy penguins bathing in the sun,
One got burnt, then there was one.

One lonely penguin weighs a mighty tonne,
He ate too much then there was none.

Emily Jeffries & Whitney May (10)
Gooderstone CE (VA) Primary School, King's Lynn

Penguin Times Tables

Two ones are two,
Penguins feet turn blue.

Two twos are four,
Tired penguins snore.

Two threes are six,
Penguins eat Weetabix.

Two fours are eight,
Penguins stay out late.

Two fives are ten,
Is that penguin Ben?

Two sixes are twelve,
Penguins dig and delve.

Two sevens are fourteen,
Penguins eat a runner bean.

Two eights are sixteen,
This penguin is really mean.

Two nines are eighteen,
Penguin crime has been seen.

Two tens are twenty,
I caught a penguin sipping plenty.

Alisha Reeves (9) & Emma Hill (10)
Gooderstone CE (VA) Primary School, King's Lynn

If I Were A Shape

If I was a shape
I'd be a sphere,
I'd be a football being smashed in the net,
I'd be a marble rolling along smooth slippery floor,
I'd be a bell jingling in a noisy band,
If I were a sphere.

I'd be a cylinder,
I'd be a pen pot filled with felt tip pens,
I'd be a swirling tunnel in a swimming pool,
I'd be a whiteboard pen writing my name,
If I were a cylinder.

I'd be a cube
I'd be a Rubix cube that you can't solve,
I'd be a jack-in-the-box when it springs up, *boo!*
I'd be a dice winning the six,
If I was a cube.
But if I were a star I'd be Diddier Drogba.

Zachary McCallum (9)
Gooderstone CE (VA) Primary School, King's Lynn

If I Were A Shape

If I were a shape
I'd be a sphere
I'd be a football that scored the winning goal
I'd be a crystal ball that saw the future
I'd be a pumpkin at Halloween
If I were a sphere

If I were a square
I'd be an ice cube on a hot summer's day
I'd be an invite to a really cool party
I'd be a potato waffle all covered in sauce
If I were a square

If I were a cylinder
I'd be a straw slurping my favourite drink
I'd be a pipe that carried water to millions
I'd be a yummy packet of biscuits
If I were a cylinder

But I am a perfect shape
Because I'm me.

Josh Hayhoe (9)
Gooderstone CE (VA) Primary School, King's Lynn

If I Were A Shape

If I were a shape
I'd be a cube,
I'd be a Rubix cube nearly about to be solved,
I'd be a special dice rolling two after Park Lane
And landing on Mayfair and buying hotels,
I'd be an ice cube cooling someone's drinks down,
If I were a cube.

If I were a pyramid,
I'd be the Eiffel Tower visited by thousands of people,
I'd be an icicle melting in the sun after winter,
I'd be a wasp sting in someone's face when they annoy me,
If I were a pyramid.

If I were a cylinder,
I'd be a bullet in a gun aimed at a bird,
I'd be the biggest canned drink in the world,
I'd be a whiteboard pen which never ran out of ink,
If I were a cylinder.

But if I were a star . . .
I'd be Nicolas Anelka!

Alfie Alexander Burge (9)
Gooderstone CE (VA) Primary School, King's Lynn

If I Were A Shape

If I were a shape
I'd be a sphere,
I'd be a football waiting to be kicked into the net by Steven Gerrard,
I'd be a cricket ball bowled at 90mph, getting a Pakistan batter out,
I'd be a bouncy ball being launched up into the sky,
If I were a sphere.

If I were a shape
I'd be a cylinder,
I'd be a bullet locked and loaded into a gun,
I'd be a tunnel, screaming cars sound out loudly,
I'd be a baked bean tin waiting to be opened and gobbled,
If I were a cylinder.

If I were a cube
I'd be a Rubix cube trying to be solved,
I'd be a box of chocolates unwrapped, melting in your mouth,
I'd be a Monopoly dice always getting sixes,
If I were a cube.

If I were a star
I'd be Eminem.

Robert Jestico (9)
Gooderstone CE (VA) Primary School, King's Lynn

If I Were A Shape

If I were a shape
I'd be a cone,
I'd be an old wizard's hat sitting on a chair near a magical wand with a frog underneath,
I'd be a blob of vanilla ice cream dripping in the sun,
I'd be a bird's beak tweeting all day long, sitting in a tree,
If I were a cone.

If I were a cube,
I'd be a big box of dark chocolates melting in your mouth,
I'd be a jack-in-a-box exploding into the air,
I'd be an ice cube sparkling in the sun,
If I were a cube.

If I were a circle,
I'd be a white plate waiting to be spun,
I'd be a chocolate cake smothered in multicoloured sweets,
I'd be a clock face ticking all day long,
If I were a circle.

But if I were a star . . .
I'd be Cheryl Cole!

Briony Clark (9)
Gooderstone CE (VA) Primary School, King's Lynn

If I Were A Shape

If I were a shape
I'd be a circle,
I'd be a base drum booming when I'm hit,
I'd be a golden button on a magician's cloak,
I'd be a ten foot tall wedding cake nobody could resist,
If I were a circle.

If I were a cube,
I'd be an enticing box of chocolates melting in your mouth,
I'd be an ice cube diving into someone's refreshing pina colada,
I'd be a bird box with a robin family nesting in me,
If I were a cube.

If I were a cylinder,
I'd be a tube of Smarties exploding with mystical colours,
I'd be a tunnel floodlit with dull orangey lights,
I'd be a roll of wrapping paper unravelling and making a wonderful gift,
If I were a cylinder.

But if I were a star . . .
I'd be shooting through the night sky.

Hannah Gamble (10)
Gooderstone CE (VA) Primary School, King's Lynn

If I Were A Shape

If I were a shape
I'd be a cube,
I'd be an ice cube chilling Steve Davies' lemon water,
I'd be a dice winning the last throw,
I'd be a jack-in-the-box surprising every kid as they wind me up,
If I were a cube.

I'd be a cylinder,
I'd be a drum banging out to the music,
I'd be a bullet hitting the clay pigeons every time,
I'd be a flowerpot holding beautiful and colourful lilies,
If I were a cylinder.

I'd be a sphere,
I'd be a cold snowball sloshing in someone's face,
I'd be a space hopper bouncing into the lead,
I'd be a marble whirling down a marble track,
If I were a sphere.

If I were a star,
I'd be Michael Johnson.

Kieran D'Aeth (10)
Gooderstone CE (VA) Primary School, King's Lynn

If I Were A Shape

If I were a shape
I'd be a cube,
I'd be a Rubix cube that could never be solved,
I'd be a dice that always landed on six,
I'd be a box of chocolates that you could never finish,
If I were a cube.

If I were a cylinder,
I'd be the biggest baked bean tin in the world,
I'd be a whiteboard pen that never runs out of ink,
I'd be a bin filled up with stinky banana skins,
If I were a cylinder.

If I were a cone,
I'd be a vampire's tooth that always needed a filling,
I'd be a nose of a rocket going to Mars,
I'd be the end of a horrid witch's pointy, long nose,
If I were a cone.

But if I were a star . . .
I'd be Jermaine Defoe!

Samuel Gilbert (9)
Gooderstone CE (VA) Primary School, King's Lynn

If I Were A Shape

If I were a shape
I'd be a cube,
I'd be a box of chocolate, melting and oozing everywhere,
I'd be an ice cube glistening and shining in the warm sun,
I'd be a Rubix cube, my puzzle impossible,
If I were a cube.

If I were a sphere
I'd be the moon twirling around the Earth,
I'd be a basketball sliding through the hoop,
I'd be an apple, very juicy and red,
If I were a sphere.

If I were a cylinder
I'd be a battery powering up a speedy sports car,
I'd be a pencil weaving in the words,
I'd be a tube of Smarties shaking about,
If I were a cylinder.

But if I were a star . . .
I'd be Eeyore.

Alisha Reeves (9)
Gooderstone CE (VA) Primary School, King's Lynn

If I Were A Shape

If I were a shape
I'd be a cone,
I'd be a blue tent for many people to camp in,
I'd be a chocolate chip ice cream that never melts,
I'd be a wizard's hat with stars all over it,
If I were a cone.

I'd be a triangle,
I'd be a kite spinning and swirling in the breeze,
I'd be a road sign showing colourful cars the way to go,
I'd be a red flag at a noisy party,
If I were a triangle.

I'd be a cube
I'd be a golden shiny box with an excellent gift inside,
I'd be an ice cube melting into freezy, frosty, sparkly water,
I'd be a silver TV showing all kinds of shows,
If I was a cube.

But if I were a star . . .
I'd be Tigger.

Emma Hill (10)
Gooderstone CE (VA) Primary School, King's Lynn

If I Were A Shape

If I were a shape
I'd be a pyramid,
I'd be a wasp's sting ready to sting anyone who dares to come too close,
I'd be the Eiffel Tower waiting for people to fuss over me,
I'd be the biggest and most famous mountain,
If I were a pyramid.

I'd be a cone,
I'd be an ice cream cone with the most wonderful flavours,
I'd be a talking wizard's hat giving everyone my spells,
I'd be a vampire's tooth ready to sink into flesh,
If I were a cone.

I'd be a circle,
I'd be a plate packed with delicious food,
I'd be a clock face telling everybody the time,
I'd be a chocolate cake melting in your mouth,
If I were a circle.

But if I were a star . . .
I'd be Miley Cyrus.

Jessica Scrivener (9)
Gooderstone CE (VA) Primary School, King's Lynn

FEATURED
AUTHOR:

MADDIE STEWART

Maddie is a children's writer, poet and author who currently lives in Coney Island, Northern Ireland.

Maddie has 5 published children's books, 'Cinders', 'Hal's Sleepover', 'Bertie Rooster', 'Peg' and 'Clever Daddy'. Maddie uses her own unpublished work to provide entertaining, interactive poems and rhyming stories for use in her workshops with children when she visits schools, libraries, arts centres and book festivals. Favourites are 'Silly Billy, Auntie Millie' and 'I'm a Cool, Cool Kid'. Maddie works throughout Ireland from her home in County Down. She is also happy to work from a variety of bases in England. She has friends and family, with whom she regularly stays, in Leicester, Bedford, London and Ashford (Kent). Maddie's workshops are aimed at 5-11-year-olds. Check out Maddie's website for all her latest news and free poetry resources **www.maddiestewart.com**.

Read on to pick up
some fab writing tips!

NONSENSE WORKSHOP

**If you find silliness fun,
you will love nonsense poems.
Nonsense poems might describe silly things,
or people, or situations,
or, any combination of the three.**

For example:

When I got out of bed today,
both my arms had run away.
I sent my feet to fetch them back.
When they came back, toe in hand
I realised what they had planned.
They'd made the breakfast I love most,
buttered spider's eggs on toast.

**One way to find out if you enjoy nonsense poems
is to start with familiar nursery rhymes.
Ask your teacher to read them out,
putting in the names of some children in your class.**

Like this: Troy and Jill went up the hill
to fetch a pail of water.
Troy fell down
and broke his crown
and Jill came tumbling after.

If anyone is upset at the idea of using their name, then don't use it.

Did you find this fun?

Now try changing a nursery rhyme.
Keep the rhythm and the rhyme style, but invent a silly situation.

Like this: Hickory Dickory Dare
a pig flew up in the air.
The clouds above
gave him a shove
Hickory Dickory Dare.

Or this: Little Miss Mabel
sat at her table
eating a strawberry pie
but a big, hairy beast
stole her strawberry feast
and made poor little Mabel cry.

How does your rhyme sound if you put your own name in it?

Another idea for nonsense poems is to pretend letters are people
and have them do silly things.

For example:

Mrs A	Mrs B	Mrs C
Lost her way	Dropped a pea	Ate a tree

To make your own 'Silly People Poem', think of a word to use.
To show you an example, I will choose the word 'silly'.
Write your word vertically down the left hand side of your page.
Then write down some words which rhyme
with the sound of each letter.

S mess, dress, Bess, chess, cress
I eye, bye, sky, guy, pie, sky
L sell, bell, shell, tell, swell, well
L " " " " " " (" means the same as written above)
Y (the same words as those rhyming with I)

Use your rhyming word lists to help you make up your poem.

Mrs S made a mess
Mrs I ate a pie
Mrs L rang a bell
Mrs L broke a shell
Mrs Y said 'Bye-bye.'

You might even make a 'Silly Alphabet' by using
all the letters of the alphabet.

It is hard to find rhyming words for all the letters.
H, X and W are letters which are hard to match with rhyming words.
I'll give you some I've thought of:

H - cage, stage, wage (close but not perfect)
X - flex, specs, complex, Middlesex
W - trouble you, chicken coop, bubble zoo

However, with nonsense poems, you can use nonsense words.
You can make up your own words.

To start making up nonsense words you could
try mixing dictionary words together.
Let's make up some nonsense animals.

Make two lists of animals. (You can include birds and fish as well.)

Your lists can be as long as you like. These are lists I made:

elephant	kangaroo
tiger	penguin
lizard	octopus
monkey	chicken

Now use the start of an animal on one list and substitute
it for the start of an animal from your other list.

I might use the start of oct/opus … oct and substitute it for the end of l/izard
to give me a new nonsense animal … an octizard.
I might swap the start of monk/ey … monk with the end of kang/aroo
To give me another new nonsense animal … a monkaroo.

What might a monkaroo look like? What might it eat?

You could try mixing some food words in the same way,
to make up nonsense foods.

cabbage	potatoes
lettuce	parsley
bacon	crisps

Cribbage, bacley, and lettatoes are some nonsense foods
made up from my lists.

Let's see if I can make a nonsense poem about my monkaroo.

84

My monkaroo loves bacley.
He'll eat lettatoes too
But his favourite food is cribbage
Especially if it's blue.

Would you like to try and make up your own nonsense poem?

**Nonsense words don't have to be a combination of dictionary words.
They can be completely 'made up'.
You can use nonsense words to write nonsense sonnets,
or list poems or any type of poem you like.**

Here is a poem full of nonsense words:

I melly micked a turdle
and flecked a pendril's tum.
I plotineyed a shugat
and dracked a pipin's plum.

**Ask your teacher to read it putting in some children's names instead
of the first I, and he or she instead of the second I.**

Did that sound funny?

You might think that nonsense poems are just silly and not for the serious poet.
However poets tend to love language. Making up your own words is a natural
part of enjoying words and sounds and how they fit together. Many poets love the
freedom nonsense poems give them. Lots and lots of very famous poets have written
nonsense poems. I'll name some: **Edward Lear**, **Roger McGough**, **Lewis Carroll**,
Jack Prelutsky and **Nick Toczek**. Can you or your teacher think of any more?
For help with a class nonsense poem or to find more nonsense nursery rhymes look
on my website, **www.maddiestewart.com**. Have fun! Maddie Stewart.

POETIC TECHNIQUES

HERE IS a SELECTION OF POETRY TECHNIQUES WITH EXAMPLES

Metaphors & Similes

A *metaphor* is when you describe your subject *as* something else, for example:
'Winter is a cruel master leaving the servants in a bleak wilderness'
whereas a *simile* describes your subject *like* something else i.e.
'His blue eyes are like ice-cold puddles' or 'The flames flickered like eyelashes'.

Personification

This is to simply give a personality to something that is not human, for example
'Fear spreads her uneasiness around' or 'Summer casts down her warm sunrays'.

Imagery

To use words to create mental pictures of what you are trying to convey,
your poem should awaken the senses and make the reader
feel like they are in that poetic scene …
'The sky was streaked with pink and red as shadows
cast across the once-golden sand'.
'The sea gently lapped the shore as the palm trees rustled softly
in the evening breeze'.

Assonance & Alliteration

Alliteration uses a repeated constant sound and this effect can be quite striking:
'Smash, slippery snake slithered sideways'.
Assonance repeats a significant vowel or vowel sound to create an impact:
'The pool looked cool'.

Repetition

By repeating a significant word the echo effect can be a very powerful way of enhancing an emotion or point your poem is putting across.
'The blows rained down, down,
Never ceasing,
Never caring
About the pain,
The pain'.

Onomatopoeia

This simply means you use words that sound like the noise you are describing, for example 'The rain *pattered* on the window' or 'The tin can *clattered* up the alley'.

Rhythm & Metre

The *rhythm* of a poem means 'the beat', the sense of movement you create. The placing of punctuation and the use of syllables affect the *rhythm* of the poem. If your intention is to have your poem read slowly, use double, triple or larger syllables and punctuate more often, where as if you want to have a fast-paced read use single syllables, less punctuation and shorter sentences. If you have a regular rhythm throughout your poem this is known as *metre*.

Enjambment

This means you don't use punctuation at the end of your line, you simply let the line flow on to the next one. It is commonly used and is a good word to drop into your homework!

Tone & Lyric

The poet's intention is expressed through their *tone*. You may feel happiness, anger, confusion, loathing or admiration for your poetic subject. Are you criticising or praising? How you feel about your topic will affect your choice of words and therefore your *tone*. For example 'I *loved* her', 'I *cared* for her', 'I *liked* her'. If you write the poem from a personal view or experience this is referred to as a *lyrical* poem. A good example of a lyrical poem is Seamus Heaney's 'Mid-term Break' or any sonnet!

All About Shakespeare

Try this fun quiz with your family, friends or even in class!

1. Where was Shakespeare born?

....

2. Mercutio is a character in which Shakepeare play?

....

3. Which monarch was said to be 'quite a fan' of his work?

....

4. How old was he when he married?

....

5. What is the name of the last and 'only original' play he wrote?

....

6. What are the names of King Lear's three daughters?

....

7. Who is Anne Hathaway?

....

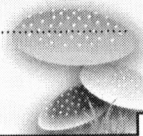

8. Which city is the play 'Othello' set in?

....

9. Can you name 2 of Shakespeare's 17 comedies?

....

10. 'This day is call'd the feast of Crispian: He that outlives this day, and comes safe home, Will stand a tip-toe when this day is nam'd, and rouse him at the name of Crispian' is a quote from which play?

....

11. Leonardo DiCaprio played Romeo in the modern day film version of Romeo and Juliet. Who played Juliet in the movie?

....

12. Three witches famously appear in which play?

....

13. Which famous Shakespearean character is Eric in the image to the left?

....

14. What was Shakespeare's favourite poetic form?

....

Answers are printed on the last page of the book, good luck!

If you would rather try the quiz online,
you can do so at www.youngwriters.co.uk.

Poetry Activity

Word Soup

To help you write a poem, or even a story, on any theme, you should create word soup!

If you have a theme or subject for your poem, base your word soup on it. If not, don't worry, the word soup will help you find a theme.

To start your word soup you need ingredients:

- Nouns (names of people, places, objects, feelings, i.e. Mum, Paris, house, anger)
- Colours
- Verbs ('doing words', i.e. kicking, laughing, running, falling, smiling)
- Adjectives (words that describe nouns, i.e. tall, hairy, hollow, smelly, angelic)

We suggest at least 5 of each from the above list, this will make sure your word soup has plenty of choice. Now, if you have already been given a theme or title for your poem, base your ingredients on this. If you have no idea what to write about, write down whatever you like, or ask a teacher or family member to give you a theme to write about.

Making Word Soup

Next, you'll need a sheet of paper.
Cut it into at least 20 pieces. Make sure the pieces are big enough to write your
ingredients on, one ingredient on each piece of paper.
Write your ingredients on the pieces of paper.
Shuffle the pieces of paper and put them all in a box or bowl
- something you can pick the paper out of without looking at the words.
Pick out 5 words to start and use them to write your poem!

Example:

Our theme is winter. Our ingredients are:
• Nouns: snowflake, Santa, hat, Christmas, snowman.
• Colours: blue, white, green, orange, red.
• Verbs: ice-skating, playing, laughing, smiling, wrapping.
• Adjectives: cold, tall, fast, crunchy, sparkly.

**Our word soup gave us these 5 words:
snowman, red, cold, hat, fast and our poem goes like this:**

It's a *cold* winter's day,
My nose and cheeks are *red*
As I'm outside, building my *snowman*,
I add a *hat* and a carrot nose to finish,
I hope he doesn't melt too *fast*!

**Tip: add more ingredients to your word soup
and see how many different poems you can write!**

**Tip: if you're finding it hard to write a poem with
the words you've picked, swap a word with another one!**

**Tip: try adding poem styles and techniques,
such as assonance or haiku to your soup for an added challenge!**

SCRIBBLER!

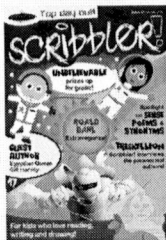

Grammar Fun
Our resident dinosaur Bernard helps to improve writing skills from punctuation to spelling.

Nessie's Workshop
Each issue Nessie explains a style of writing and sets an exercise for you to do. Previous workshops include the limerick, haiku and shape poems.

Awesome Author
Read all about past and present authors. Previous Awesome Authors include Roald Dahl, William Shakespeare and Ricky Gervais!

Once Upon a Time …
Lord Oscar starts a story … it's your job to finish it. Our favourite wins a writing set.

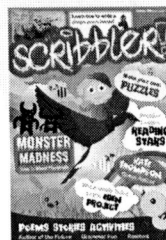

Guest Author
A famous author drops by and answers some of our in-depth questions, while donating a great prize to give away. Recent authors include former Children's Laureate Michael Morpurgo, adventurer Bear Grylls and Nick Ward, author of the Charlie Small Journals.

Art Gallery
Send Bizzy your paintings and drawings and his favourite wins an art set including some fab Staedtler goodies.

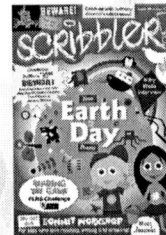

Puzzle Time!
Could you find Eric? Unscramble Anna Gram's words? Tackle our hard puzzles? If so, winners receive fab prizes.

The Brainiacs
Scribbler!'s own gang of wiz kids are always on hand to help with spellings, alternative words and writing styles, they'll get you on the right track!

Prizes
Every issue we give away fantastic prizes. Recent prizes include Staedtler goodies, signed copies of Bear Grylls' books and posters, signed copies of Ricky Gervais' books, Charlie Small goodie bags, family tickets to The Eden Project, The Roald Dahl Museum & Story Centre and Alton Towers, a digital camera, books and writing sets galore and many other fab prizes!

... plus much more!
We keep you up to date with all the happenings in the world of literature, including blog updates from the Children's Laureate.

If I Were A Shape

If I were a shape
I'd be a cube,
I'd be a winning red dice rolling around the colourful snakes and ladders,
I'd be a Rubix cube, confusing and hypnotising people
In a flash of bright colours,
I'd be an ice cube shining in the hot sun
While floating about in sweet lemonade,
If I were a cube.

I'd be a cone,
I'd be a tornado thrashing around, hoovering everything in its way,
I'd be a tip of a pencil scribbling away frantically,
I'd be a wigwam tent next to a crackling, blazing fire,
If I were a cone.

I'd be a cylinder,
I'd be a killer bullet flying through the air,
I'd be a tin of baked beans being poured onto thick, crunchy toast,
I'd be a Maypole surrounded by swirling whirling ribbons,
If I were a cylinder.

But if I were a star . . .
I'd be twinkling in the moonlight.

Emily Jeffries (10)
Gooderstone CE (VA) Primary School, King's Lynn

If I Were A Shape

If I were a shape
I'd be a circle,
I'd be a wheel on a beautiful Aston Martin,
I'd be a pancake waiting for sticky, syrupy toppings - delicious!
I'd be a clock face telling the time to people without watches,
If I were a circle.

If I were a sphere,
I'd be a cricket ball waiting for Graeme Swann to bowl at the stumps,
I'd be a bowling ball waiting to get a strike - 300 points!
I'd be a scoop of ice cream perfectly round and soft - yummy!
If I were a sphere.

If I were a cylinder,
I'd be a baked bean tin to be eaten by starving people,
I'd be a bullet that is so powerful that it could blow up tanks,
I'd be a whiteboard pen drawing a picture,
If I were a cylinder.

If I were a star . . .
I'd be Stuart Broad!

Nicholas Morgan (11)
Gooderstone CE (VA) Primary School, King's Lynn

My Singing Habit!

I sing all night, I sing all day,
To get my troubles far away,
I sing at school, I sing at home,
I sing when the day is done!
I sing in the science room,
I sing when the news is on,
I should see a doctor about this,
My singing habit's in a twist!
As you see it is clear to me,
Singing's here to stay with me!

I'm going to sing for all my life,
Until the very day I die,
I will become the biggest star,
The greatest ever superstar!

Hannah Pegram (10)
Heron Primary School, Abbeydale

Pizza, Pizza

Pizza, pizza on the plate
The thicker the crust
The better the taste.

Pizza, pizza like a frisbee
It tastes just great
Just thin and crispy!

Pizza, pizza round and flat
Not too much cheese
Or you'll get fat!

Pizza, pizza it tastes great
The final thing is
To fill your face!

Tyler Martin (10)
Heron Primary School, Abbeydale

Bubble Wrap

You hear it from the father,
You hear it from the son,
Bubble wrap, bubble wrap,
It's always fun!

Bubble wrap, bubble wrap,
Hear it pop,
Bubble wrap, bubble wrap,
Pop till you drop!

Bubble wrap, bubble wrap,
Never miss out,
Bubble wrap, bubble wrap,
Give a big shout!

Ben McLean (10)
Heron Primary School, Abbeydale

The Tiger!

A tiger has stripes,
Which lay him bare,
You really can't see him,
But you know that he's there.

A growl and a roar,
This animal's a beast,
To catch a wild antelope,
Upon it he would feast.

Tigers are wild,
Certainly not tame
But for killing Man,
They are not to blame.

From Bengal to Africa,
They are all the same,
Stalked by Man,
And treated as game.

Hunted and tortured,
For trophies they are sought,
For trading in markets,
Where their skin can be bought.

Now their numbers are so few,
With total destruction they are linked,
We must act now,
Before they are extinct!

Jack Rees (10)
Heron Primary School, Abbeydale

The Winning Try

'Gloucester, Gloucester!' cheered the chanting, capacity crowd.
I joined in and it made me feel proud.
The referee blew his whistle, it was the start of the match.
Robinson kicked off and Brown took a clean catch.
He went to ground and the forwards formed a ruck,
Wasps roared like lions but got their feet stuck.
Dave Lewis captured the ball and made a pass.
Nicky Robinson kicked the ball and it landed on the soft, spongy grass.
Sinbad chased like a cheetah and snatched it up.
He dived over the line, 'We're going to win the Cup.'
'Gloucester, Gloucester!' cheered the chanting, capacity crowd.
I joined in and it made me feel proud.

James Harris (10)
Heron Primary School, Abbeydale

Tiger At Heart

In the day he's sweet and cute,
At night he turns, becomes a brute
And whilst we're fast asleep at night
In the dark his prey's in sight.
Frogs are easy; their croak is heard,
The beast creeps up without a word.
Mice are quick but so's the killer,
The chase soon becomes a thriller.
So through this tale you may see
That a tiger at heart is he.

Natasha Stewart (10)
Heron Primary School, Abbeydale

Sweet Surprise!

Lollipops and candy sticks
Haribos and pick 'n' mix
Sour ones and plain ones too
Some you suck and some you chew
Cola bottles, jelly beans
Afterwards your teeth you clean

Dairy Milk and Galaxy
KitKat, Crunchie and Bounty
Plain, dark, milk, the choice is yours
I am off to eat some more.

Kayleigh Clarke (10)
Heron Primary School, Abbeydale

Free!

I'm trapped, oh no what can I do?
It's life, it's work, I'm captured by you
What can I do? I'm like a puppet to you
These troubles must escape from me
I'm living my life for you not for me
I need to add my own style, my own touch
Help me, help me, help me to be free.

Dani Miles (10)
Heron Primary School, Abbeydale

Creatures Of The Night

Down in the woods on a moonlit night,
If you're very still and quiet,
You might see a flash of black and white.
Down in the woods on a moonlit night,
You might see sturdy feet,
Digging in the soil for a snack to eat.
Roots are good but you really can't beat
Worms and bugs for a tasty treat.
Down in the woods on a moonlit night,
Badgers roam in the silver light.
They sleep all day when the sun is bright
But the woods are theirs in the silence of the night.

Emily Phillips (10)
Heron Primary School, Abbeydale

My Pet Rabbit Nibbles

I have a pet rabbit,
He answers to Nibbles,
He drinks a lot,
But sometimes dribbles.

He mainly lives in a cage,
It's made out of wood,
He tries to get out,
And would jump at the chance if he could.

Hopping around the garden,
He has so much to see,
Near the flowers and shrubs,
Or even the tree.

I have a wonderful rabbit,
Who is the very best,
And I stroke and tickle,
His fluffy, white chest.

Chloe Bird (10)
Heron Primary School, Abbeydale

The Rainbows

The rainbows shine with all the colours.
Beautiful as the sun comes out.
Listening to the raindrops pitter-patter.
When the sun comes we say goodbye to the rain.
The colourful rainbow always means that the rain is gone.

Ruponeso Mapanga (8)
Kirkstall Valley Primary School, Leeds

School Poem

The birds are tweeting and the sun is beaming
But the silly girl keeps on screaming!
Playtime is finished so now the teacher has to prepare
For her next session
But the children think it's torture to do loads of lessons.
Girls think we are gonna do history next
But the boys keep moaning, 'Can we have a rest?'

Joseph Aaron (11)
Kirkstall Valley Primary School, Leeds

In The Park

Big fluffy clouds high in the blue clear sky.
White swans floating in the beautiful lake nearby.
Children relaxing and having fun.
Adults cheering that their housework is done.
Birds are saying *tweet tweet tweet*.
Wow their songs are so sweet.

Humairaa Mahmood (10)
Kirkstall Valley Primary School, Leeds

Motorbike - The Day Of My Life

The rising of the waking sun,
The signal a new day has begun.
The birds start tweeting
And I'm waiting to get on the scarlet red motorbike.
I jump on and hold on, and happily wait till the engine starts
And I have the ride of my life.
Off to the seaside we are going,
I wonder if the wind is blow, blow, blowing.

Sophie Kaye (10)
Kirkstall Valley Primary School, Leeds

The Midnight Fox

Camouflaged between dull rocks,
Black as coal with white tips,
Pouncing and bouncing through the ravine,
Shimmering her green, glowing dagger eyes,
This beautiful endangered creature sneakily uses her brains.

This ravenous vixen creeps through the shiny green grass,
Silently, the cunning fox swims through the bushes,
Cute, cuddly, the midnight fox.

The greedy animal spots a mouse,
Within a minute it is in her jaws,
Her pointed ears aware,
She sniffs and listens with great care.

She sneaks upon a scarecrow,
Although nothing gives her a scare,
The field is clear of crows,
Now the crops fill the field,
Except for the fox's paw prints,
Bold, rare and harmless,
The midnight fox.

Isobel Salter (10)
Lapal Primary School, Halesowen

Is It That Time Already?

I really don't want to leave my little school,
Can't tell anyone, they'd think I'm such a fool.
The forms are here,
I've only got one year.
Let's look around and around,
This week my feet haven't touched the ground.

Oh my God this one is fab,
Libraries, pools and science lab.
Second one not so good,
Really can't go here,
I just don't think I should.
Presentations, microphones, head teachers dressed in suits,
Over-diluted cordial of non-descriptive fruits!

Need to choose the one that's right for me.
Only another 500 to see!
Well, that's how it feels anyway,
So no more to say.
Time to move, it's such a shame,
At least happy memories will remain.

George Arthur Sheppard (10)
Lapal Primary School, Halesowen

My Little Caterpillar

Caterpillar in the tree.
Wondering what you will be.
One day you will become a pretty butterfly.
Butterfly fly away.

Dabrina Forrester (9)
Lintonmead Primary School, Thamesmead

My Chickens

I have five little chickens
Running round my garden
Pecking up soil
Scratching up my garden
Laying big brown eggs
For me and my daddy's breakfast in the morning
Claira *cluck, cluck* and *cluck* and *clucks*
Until she sees her friends the ducks
The ducks go *quack*
The chickens go *cluck*
All day long they play in muck.

Coby Stringer (7)
North Reddish Junior School, North Reddish

Fox And The Hen

Mr Fox was hiding behind a box
He was watching the hen
Dancing in its pen
Fox crept up to the pen
But then . . .
Bang! Bang!
Went the farmer's gun
And oh how that fox did run!

Alex Liston (7)
North Reddish Junior School, North Reddish

Untitled

The bombs are dropping.
The Blitz has started.
Evacuees fill the station.
The train pulls into the station.
The soldiers march through the town.

Jack Beeby (8)
North Reddish Junior School, North Reddish

The Blitz

Lots of bombs are dropped by aeroplanes.
They make craters and cause destruction.
The sirens wail day and night,
While the soldiers fight, fight, fight!

Alexander Dean (8)
North Reddish Junior School, North Reddish

Untitled

There are many memories of the war
Of all the things I heard and saw.
The sirens went on more every day
The evacuees' trains, also buses were moving on one road.
The other children moved to the countryside
To be safe from the Blitz.
Adults stayed in the cities,
At night they hid in the air raid shelter to sleep overnight.
They had beds in the air raid shelters
And they took their gas masks.

Ellie Kitchen (9)
North Reddish Junior School, North Reddish

Memories

I have many memories of the war,
Of all the things I heard and saw.
Hitler the bully
And children going to the lovely countryside
To be safe from the Blitz.
Me fighting for my country.

George Moss (9)
North Reddish Junior School, North Reddish

Untitled

I have many memories of the war
Of all the things I heard and saw.

Children moved to the countryside,
To be safe from the Blitz.

Adults stayed in the cities,
At night they hid in the shelters.

Riah Hughes (8)
North Reddish Junior School, North Reddish

Untitled

The bombs were dropping
The Blitz had started
Evacuees crowded the platform
The train pulled into the station
Soldiers marched through the streets.

Ibraheem Khuram (8)
North Reddish Junior School, North Reddish

Untitled

I have many memories of the war
Of all the things that I heard and saw.
The bombs came fast.
We ran to hide for our lives,
Over to the air raid shelters
To save our lives.
In the morning
We got up to the horrible sight.
Fire and the place a wreck,
It was a sad sight to see.

Madelane Bean (8)
North Reddish Junior School, North Reddish

WWII

When I was in the war,
There were many rules in the law.
Spitfires, Hurricanes zooming past,
Evacuees had gone at last.
Women taking over men's jobs,
People hiding in the Anderson shelters
Or air raid shelters, scared of the Blitz.
The barrage balloons' metal wires
Chopping off the German planes' wings.
Finally the war ended in 1945
V E Day had come (Victory in Europe Day).

Ellis Breen (8)
North Reddish Junior School, North Reddish

Untitled

Lots of people dropped bombs
And some bombs landed on people's houses
Many people died in 1939
War ended in 1945
Many, many people were killed by guns.

Mason Hamilton (8)
North Reddish Junior School, North Reddish

World War II

I have many memories of the war,
Of all the things I heard and saw.
I saw lots of bombs dropped by aeroplanes.
The Blitz started and I was really scared,
We all ran to the Anderson shelter,
In the morning we came out of the shelters
And cleaned the mess up.

Kharina Simmonds (8)
North Reddish Junior School, North Reddish

WWII

I have many memories of the war,
Of all the things I heard and saw.
The bombs are dropping,
The Blitz has started.
Spitfires going,
Evacuees going to the countryside.
All of the parents are very upset,
Their children are crying.

Amelia Bright (8)
North Reddish Junior School, North Reddish

Untitled

The bombs are dropping
The Blitz has started
Evacuees crowd the platform
The train pulls into the station
Soldiers march through streets
Everyone cheers, V E Day is here.

Connie Clews (8)
North Reddish Junior School, North Reddish

War Memories

I have many memories of the war,
Of all the things I heard and saw.
The bombs are dropping,
The Blitz has started.
While Hitler is working,
Winston Churchill is resting.
Bombs are working, while people are turning.
Evacuees are going, while soldiers are coming.
More gas masks are coming, while people are going.
Medals are going while people are in the shelters.

Ellie Blackwood (8)
North Reddish Junior School, North Reddish

Memories Of War

I have many memories
of the war planes flying overhead,
bombs dropping everywhere,
planes crashing, clanging,
the world coming to an end.

James Martlew (9)
North Reddish Junior School, North Reddish

The Seed

Here is a seed
Shiny and round
Ready to grow
Not being drowned
Here is the sun and rain
To help it flower
They will give it power
Now it is beautiful
We can admire its beauty.

Leo Barontini (7)
Quinton Primary School, Stratford upon Avon

In The Sky

In the sky
Geese passed by,
When I went to say hello
My baby sister said, 'Yellow.'

I like the sunset
Because I bet,
That there's nothing better than you could see,
Not even a pretty flower with a bumblebee.

Clouds look so fluffy,
Do they know Duffy?
Sometimes they look so dark,
Maybe they will start to bark.

All the stars
Eat chocolate bars,
It's not fair,
They should share.

Lucy Griffiths (10)
Quinton Primary School, Stratford upon Avon

Bullies

Bullies are mean and can make you very sad,
I had an experience and it was the worst time I had,
Most bullies are just trying to put on a show,
But that's not the right way to go,
Nice people have lots of good friends,
So if you want to be liked,
Make sure all bullying ends.

Holly Ibrahim (8)
Rodmersham Primary School, Sittingbourne

Me

I am Samuel
I have two hamsters called Rafy and Rodgey
But are not podgy
I am a loon
But I do not jump over the moon!
I am a good friend
The end.

Samuel May (9)
Rodmersham Primary School, Sittingbourne

My Best Friends

I like to run, I like to play,
I like to go to school every day.
I just can't wait to see my friends,
Sometimes they drive me round the bend.
We laugh, we joke, we have so much fun,
They really are my best chums.
Birthday parties are so much fun,
Someone hit me with a bread bun.
We fell down laughing,
The party was done.

Brooke Smith (8)
Rodmersham Primary School, Sittingbourne

Heidi

My name is Heidi,
I have green eyes
And I hate flies.
I have blonde hair
And I like to run everywhere.
I like to watch telly
And I'm a bit heavy.
I like to go on the computer
And I have a scooter.

Heidi Camber (9)
Rodmersham Primary School, Sittingbourne

Coco

Coco is my cat,
She never has a chat.
One day I dropped her in a pool.
She drowned and drowned
But she leapt on a stool.
Coco is my cat,
She never has a pat.
One day she ran up in a tree,
I tried to catch her but she ran free.
Coco is my cat,
She always catches a rat!

Olivia Corder (8)
Rodmersham Primary School, Sittingbourne

I Hate Parties

I hate parties
They're always a mess
I don't know how to plan them
But then I get fed up and guess
I love party hats
I like the theme
They're always cats
You can't blame me

I know I'm badly dressed
That's why I'm late
I can't care any less
But then I have a debate
I can't lie, I like the food
I get hardly any
That puts me in a bad mood.

Now you have heard no lies
Go spill some of yours
Goodbye for now before my fame dies.

Katrina Kallu (10)
St John's Catholic Primary School, Gravesend

My Name Is Dan

My name is Dan,
I'm a cool, cool dude,
I like to eat all kinds of food.
Kentucky, McDonald's and Pizza Hut,
I really don't care, I like the lot!
A bowl full of ice cream,
A sugary doughnut or apple pie,
I'm up for everything,
I'll give them all a try!

Daniel Dartnell (10)
St John's Catholic Primary School, Gravesend

Lottie's Lanzarote

My name is Lottie,
My trip to Lanzarote,
Where the sea is sparkly and blue.
There's snorkelling, scuba-diving
And jet skiing too!
We all go shopping for bracelets and bangles,
And beads for our ankles.
Along the beach we find hermit crabs,
Ones with big shells are up for grabs!
There's places to eat and friends to meet,
Holiday-makers, pizza bakers,
All this fun, in the sun,
Snooker games that I won!
Now it's the end of the summer,
Back to school, what a bummer!

Rebecca Hill (10)
St John's Catholic Primary School, Gravesend

The Alien

When I was a teen,
I saw an alien that was green.
It had one eye,
That was as big as a pie.
It struck a pose,
And stuck out its massive nose.
Its name was Mockey
And it looked a bit like a jockey.
So it entered a race
And it won 1st place!

Lucy Hope (10)
St John's Catholic Primary School, Gravesend

My Wonderful Things Called Pets

This is the day that I meet,
These wonderful things called pets.
One big and one small,
They really are so cool.
I've got one rabbit and a dog,
They run happily together in days of fog.
My lovely dog is called Ted,
He loves to lie on his comfortable bed.
Ted is so, so cute and sweet,
He is a wonderful dog to meet.
My wonderful rabbit is called Co-Co,
He runs around like loco.
He is so tiny and fluffy,
He is a little toughie.
Sometimes you two make me yell and scream,
But come on, we are always a team.
This poem is for both of you,
So keep doing what you do.

Amie Foxcroft (10)
St John's Catholic Primary School, Gravesend

My Pup, Bentley

I have a puppy called Bentley,
And we're trying to teach him to play gently,
He is one fantastic little pup,
He likes to chew a plastic green cup,
He always uses his nose,
He even licks between your toes,
He has many brothers and sisters
And on his first walk he got quite a few blisters,
He likes you to tickle his belly,
Especially when he's watching the telly!

Madeline Simmons (10)
St John's Catholic Primary School, Gravesend

My Cat

My cat is very funny,
he likes to hunt and play,
his fur is like a bunny,
so I hug him every day.

My cat can climb a brick wall,
escaping other cats,
he likes to play with a ball,
and resting on the mat.

His eyes are very scary,
when he is in the dark,
but they are very merry,
when daytime is here at last.

My cat is very clever,
he knows me by my smell,
he will know me forever,
even when I am not well.

I'm lucky I have Felix,
he wakes me up for school,
he always knows my feelings
and Felix is no fool.

Oscar Swiatek (10)
St John's Catholic Primary School, Gravesend

My Brother Marco!

Marco, Marco, what can I say?
He plays on his Xbox every day,
Modern Warfare, Black Ops too,
He must be the gamer king,
It must be true,
He stays on it all day,
It does give us peace I must say,
That's all I've got to say,
Go on Marco, go and play.

Elena Napoliello (10)
St John's Catholic Primary School, Gravesend

Sally The Cat

Once there was a cat,
Who was brown.
She sat on the mat,
She wore a green gown.

Her name was Sally,
She chased a dog.
Down the alley,
Into a bog.

Sally liked to eat fish,
She hated milk.
Tuna was her best dish,
It made her fur like silk.

She slept on the bed,
On a comfy pillow.
Resting her tired head,
Dreaming of her favourite willow.

Luke Wilson (10)
St John's Catholic Primary School, Gravesend

S4 Girls!

We are the S4 girls, we are cool, funky and crazy
We do nothing but sing and we are lazy
The S4 girls walk around and have a lot of bling
We are funky as a dance floor and are enjoyable
When we see a guitar and a microphone we sing and play.

All we smell is candyfloss and popcorn
When we hear the beat of the drums we want to play and sing
We always love karaoke and we always like to be groovy shining stars.

Amy Ling (10)
St John's Catholic Primary School, Gravesend

Planet Wardrobe

This dark little hole, this small little place
My bedroom wardrobe, it's my one little space
Where I draw and I dream
Even eat strawberry ice cream
Teddies and dolls staring down at me
From up on the shelf, trying to see
The cat sneaks up to be by my side
Mum's coming up, Smudge quickly hides
Making a camp is always great fun
Hanging up drapes and banners to come
We all crowd into this cold tiny gap
We laugh and we giggle, but mostly we chat
Although it is cold with spiders in webs
My pictures and posters give a warm glow of red
When I'm in the camp I watch my telly
While Dad's downstairs he eats raspberry jelly
He shouts upstairs, 'It's getting late.'
I look at the clock, it's half-past eight
As I pull back my covers I think of the fun
And I start to dream there's more to come.

Megan Lorence (10)
St John's Catholic Primary School, Gravesend

School Day

Boys and girls running around
Having fun in the playground.
Mums and dads calling their names
It's time for school, not playing games.

Teachers standing at the door
Ringing the bell for evermore.
One by one, standing in line
Time to go in, the clock says nine.

First it's school assembly and then English as a class
Quickly into PE kits for footie on the grass.
Then it's maths, science and a little bit of history
Learning from the past can sometimes be a mystery.

The bell rings at half-past one
The queue is really long even though lunch has just begun.
Yummy smells wafting through the door
Children gobble up their food, asking for more.

Back to class but the day is nearly done
It will be home time soon and time for more fun.
Children singing loudly as the music lesson rocks
Playing as a band to the rhythm of the clock.

Boys and girls running around
Having fun in the playground.
Mums and dads calling their names
It's time for home, not playing games.

Amy Roberts (10)
St John's Catholic Primary School, Gravesend

Driving Home In The Rain

Driving home in the rain,
has started to become quite a pain,
the rain is splashing down,
which makes me want to frown,
the windscreen wipers swished left and right,
trying their best to put up a fight.

Driving home in the rain,
lights shine bright in the other lane,
cars swerved, trying hard to see,
with the passengers hurrying home for tea,
cats' eyes shine as we pass,
the engine purring as we glide so fast.

Driving home in the rain,
we missed the turning, oh what a shame,
we turned the car ninety degrees,
next stop is home, we're all very pleased,
I get out of the car and stretch my knees,
oh my gosh, I've lost the front door keys.

George Albert (10)
St John's Catholic Primary School, Gravesend

My Dog

I have a clumsy puppy,
Fernando is his name.
He's always tripping over things,
I think he is insane!

He is the cutest puppy,
That I have ever seen.
But always finds a way somehow,
To keep himself unclean!

Matthew McDermott (10)
St John's Catholic Primary School, Gravesend

Word Frenzy

Caring words like big red roses,
Naughty words snarl and pick their noses,
Foreign words seem lost and shrug,
Lazy words sit on the rug,
Strong words try to break the slate,
Chummy words call each other mate,
Funny words have a laugh and gabble,
Clever words have a game of Scrabble,
Now this poem has been read,
All the words shall go to bed.

Sean Timothy Matthews (10)
St John's Catholic Primary School, Gravesend

An Irish Jig For You!

Diddly, diddly doo
An Irish jig for you
Standing on the stage
I feel so proud
Looking at the crowd
The music turns on loud
My leg kicks out high
As I jump to reach to the sky
Everyone goes wow and I think I've won it now
Diddly, diddly doo
Another great Irish jig for you.

Jade Keepin (10)
St John's Catholic Primary School, Gravesend

My Dog Densil

My dog Densil loves to wrestle,
Especially when we're about to settle.
He is only a puppy, as white as snow
And is really happy as dogs go.
He has one black ear and a pig's nose
But has four paws and no toes.
He looks really scary
But is not hairy.
He is playful and fun, what a bundle of joy
And always makes sure you knock on the door!

Jack Mooney (10)
St John's Catholic Primary School, Gravesend

Dolphin Discovery

I was waiting for the playful dolphins to come.
So patiently I began to joyfully hum.
Then *whoosh!* I went up high into the air.
The dolphins pushed me with such gentle care.
Then they dropped me down, down, down . . .
I landed safely with a splashing sound.
I thought it was enormous fun.
Swimming the day away in the sizzling sun.
Soon I would love to do it all again
But unfortunately now I am sitting on a tedious plane.

Isabella Hope Webb (10)
St John's Catholic Primary School, Gravesend

What I See!

I look outside my window
And guess what I can see
A pretty little bird
Singing out for me.

I look outside my window
And guess what I can see
My neighbour's sly, old cat
Climbing up my willow tree.

I look outside my window
And guess what I can see
Floating from flower to flower
A busy, buzzy bee.

I look outside my window
And guess what I can see
My own, familiar reflection
Staring back at me.

Anna Parker (10)
St John's Catholic Primary School, Gravesend

Winter All The Time

In winter it is white and beautiful,
The ice is see-through like a glass cup,
The children are sledging down the hill
And they are falling off and rolling like a ball
And turning into a snowball.

Joseph Cox (10)
St John's Catholic Primary School, Gravesend

I Think My Nan's An Alien!

I think my nan's an alien,
I really don't know why!
I have to tell you the truth,
(Well, I can't really lie!).

I think my nan's an alien,
She gave us mushroom pie!
And when she came to me,
I said, 'I'd rather die!'

I think my nan's an alien,
She makes my sister cry!
And when she comes to feed her,
She pretends the spoon can fly!

I think my nan's an alien,
Although she's very shy!
Maybe she's not that bad,
Boom! Or not! I'll have to deny!

Isha Ahluwalia (10)
St John's Catholic Primary School, Gravesend

Aeroplanes

Aeroplanes are fast as they pass like a speeding bullet,
Onboard you can smell food and people,
You can see clouds like wool, people, videos
And you can taste food like Heaven, you can hear videos.

The air is as thin as ice, the sun is like gold as you zoom along,
As fast as a cheetah and as quiet as a mouse and touch food, seats,
Fast and quiet like a colourful, gliding bird.

They're comfortable and fluffy like a piece of cotton wool,
They're like a large aluminium tube powering through the dense air.

Samuel Hodges (10)
St John's Catholic Primary School, Gravesend

Match Of The Day

The whistle has blown,
The noise has grown,
I shout and call
Because I want that ball,
I get the ball, I hear a call,
I do a pass
Along the grass,
The player shoots
With his bright pink boots
But it doesn't go in.
It's late in the game,
Who scores gets fame,
I get the ball,
After a call.
I take it past one
But the job isn't done,
I do a dummy,
I think it's funny,
I shoot
But it hits the crossbar
And goes down,
The keeper's a clown,
It comes off his bum
And it's done,
The crowd roared,
I think I've scored.
I did all that work,
I feel like a berk
Because it's the keeper's goal!

Aran Larner (10)
St John's Catholic Primary School, Gravesend

S4 Girls

We are the S4 girls, we are fun
We are cool, we are groovy and we're crazy
We do nothing but sing and have some fun
We are also very lazy
We are as crazy as a whirlwind
We are the funniest girls you can ever imagine
When we see a guitar and microphone
We sing and play
All we smell is candyfloss and popcorn
When we hear the beat of drums
We want to sing along and play
We always love karaoke
And at night the stars come out
They're shining right upon us
That makes us feel like stars too.

Courtnay Anne Curtis (10)
St John's Catholic Primary School, Gravesend

Winter Mornings

In a winter morning
It is freezing cold
So you wrap up warm
To be nice and hot
We go outside to have fun

Snow is as cold as an ice cube
It is cold when you walk
On snow it makes your feet really cold
So you go and lie down in a nice warm bed.

Sophie Connell (10)
St John's Catholic Primary School, Gravesend

Summer

School's out.
None of us are hanging about.
Summer is here,
Time to dance and cheer.

Putting on my cossie.
Using bug spray to get rid of those mozzies.
Sitting by the pool,
Which is ice cool.

Smell the summer fruits being baked in a pie.
That will attract a load of flies.
Not so warm.
Starting to lose the mozzie swarms.

I feared this day,
Autumn is not so far away.
Summer is at an end,
Autumn is here.

Sophie Gibson (10)
St John's Catholic Primary School, Gravesend

Weather In The Winter

In the winter it is beautiful
Everyone is happy
There are silver see-through icicles
If you look around you, you can see
How wonderful winter truly is.

When I run across the white snowy field
I feel the cold wind brushing through my face
When you feel the snowball hit you your whole body shivers.

I love it when you come home and the warm fire's on
And you can smell the dinner cooking
In the distance you can see the Christmas lights.

Hollie Nicola Ludlow (10)
St John's Catholic Primary School, Gravesend

Planes And Trains

Planes are cool, they fly high, high in the sky
Over long journeys although they are slow
They are cool and they are amazing
The propellers go extremely fast
Also they can get you from country to country, now for trains . . .

Trains are fast and by fast I mean really fast
They go on a long, long way, carrying passengers
Some carrying containers with stuff in them
Trains are a good form of transport
Because they can get you from city to city.

Trains and planes are all so cool
No matter what type of plane or train it is they are all cool
From old to new, even future ones, they might be cool
As the present ones we have now.

Harry Thompson (10)
St John's Catholic Primary School, Gravesend

DDKC

My name is Dylan
I'm a cool, cool dude
And I like all kinds of food
Nandos, McDonald's and Pizza Hut
I don't care, I like the lot
So does my friend, Daniel D
Especially chicken from KFC
And Kieron HB, he's footie mad
He lives with his mum, sister, bro and dad
Oh yeah and the last of us
Cai Onraet, he'll never fuss
Yeah, that's us.

Dylan Mark Cable (10)
St John's Catholic Primary School, Gravesend

Easter Bunny

When the children sleep in the night,
Little Bunny comes to life,
He gives us sweets and bars and chocolate,
For behaving ourselves every day,
He brings happiness to us all
And the peace of course!

Weronika Brzezinska (10)
St John's Catholic Primary School, Gravesend

My Cats

Cats chase birds,
Cats chase flies,
Cats are also afraid of heights
And they always bite.

Cats are cute,
I wish I could make them mute,
They lap milk up
With a *slip, slap, sloop.*

Some cats giggle,
With a little wiggle,
They're as funny as clowns,
They're also brown.

Bethany Stevens (10)
St John's Catholic Primary School, Gravesend

A Cold Winter's Night

As the night draws cold, snowflakes start falling,
With the trees swaying and the owls cooing,
With the twinkling stars, I look in the sky,
Then a great white dove, gracefully flies by.

As I kneel to the snow it sends a shiver and I shout out, 'Cold!'
Then I pat the snow and start to roll,
Because I'm making a man that's made of snow.

As I stand up my mum opens the door,
She sends out a call saying it's late no more,
As I tootle along through the crunchy snow,
And I say to my mum, 'Do I have to go?'

Kia Lea Peek (10)
St John's Catholic Primary School, Gravesend

S4 Girls

We are the S4 girls, we are the S4 girls,
We always stick together whatever the weather,
We like to play S4 square all day long
And sing a song, we are fun, we are groovy,
We watch a movie,
All of the day, all of the night
And sometimes we give each other a scary fright!

Amy is good at art,
Courtnay is good at fashion,
Phoebe is good at dancing,
I'm good at being a friend
But when we all get together we're all good at singing,
And being there for each other no matter what,
We stick up for each other,
Sometimes we get into silly little fights
Then we are friends again but we're always there, yeah.

Toni Michelle Brook Jarvis Mitchell (10)
St John's Catholic Primary School, Gravesend

Holiday

I went on holiday to Kent
I stayed in a big blue tent
It was yellow and orange inside
In my sleeping bag I liked to hide
We ate our meals outside
Bacon and eggs, all fried
When it came to the washing up
We all tried to hide.

Georgia Long (9)
St Mary's RC Primary School, Boston

My Holiday Mexico!

I went to Mexico,
Instead of San Francisco,
As I was playing my Mexican guitar
I saw a man smoking a cigar.

I went to Mexico
Instead of Jericho,
As I was playing my maracas
Everyone started going crackers.

I went to Mexico
Instead of Acapulco,
The sun was hot, mucho, mucho,
I had to take off my poncho.
Olé.

Esme Clarricoates (9)
St Mary's RC Primary School, Boston

The Season Spring

I love the season spring
The birds they play and sing
The bees live in a tree
I don't want them to sting me
The trees blow gently in the breeze
After the long winter freeze.

Chloe Robinson (9)
St Mary's RC Primary School, Boston

Spring

At the start of the year in February,
I went to the seal sanctuary,
Where there were newborn pups,
Who could fit in little cups.

Outside the daffodils are starting to grow,
Peeping through the melting blankets of snow,
I think now you know,
Finally spring is here.

Laiba Imran (9)
St Mary's RC Primary School, Boston

On Holiday

I was in pain
When I went to Spain
I said, 'I want an ice cream,'
'What do you mean
You want an ice cream?'
Then I woke up
I had, had a dream.

Simon Layton (9)
St Mary's RC Primary School, Boston

My Family

My mum is very kind,
She has a great mind.
My dad is very strong,
He never does anything wrong.
My brother is so funny,
When he smiles he looks sunny.
My fish is very fat,
And looks like my cat.

Demi Whiting (9)
St Mary's RC Primary School, Boston

The Brain

The brain said,
'I'm not working
No way Jose
I'm feeling embarrassed
A bit pink in the face
Oh no not homework
Homework's a bore.
Please
No more
Let's fall apart
Anything but homework.'

Owen Hall (11)
St Paul's CE Primary School, Preston

A Car That Can

A car that can talk a mile a minute
A car that can hover over lakes
A car that run very fast
A car that can see through walls
A car that can stand very high
A car that can shout hello
A car that can fly like a plane
A car that can grow
A car that can turn into a Transformer
A car that can turn into a stereo
A car that can do a back flip
A car that can turn into another car
A car that can shoot a robot.

Ryan Woods (10)
St Paul's CE Primary School, Preston

A Pineapple's Insecurities - Lemon's Revenge

There once was a pineapple
Who lived on a shelf
He didn't care
About himself.

He had a friend
Called Lemon
Who was born
In Devon.

'Lemon's such a
Sour puss'
Said Pineapple
To Gus and Russ.

Pineapple and Lemon
Had a chat
Lemon said
Pineapple was fat.

Pineapple groans
And Pineapple moans
He complains about
Not being a scout!

I need a shave
I'm going seriously spiky
I'm going to look like my
Uncle Mikey.

Oh my gosh my hair's
Gone floppy.
I put gel in today
Why has it gone sloppy?

'Lemon, am I a pineapple?'
'Yes you are.
I wish you would go
Some place far.'

But that very moment
Lemon had a plan
He would scare Pineapple
And make him run to his gran!

Lemon's plan worked
Pineapple had disappeared,
This is what everybody
Had feared.

Lemon was evil
As evil as a witch
He had left poor Pineapple
In a lonely ditch.

Phoebe Bourne (10)
St Paul's CE Primary School, Preston

The Moving Car

Is a car and a person.
It can go to car school.
It can sit down.
It can speak.
The car can go to the shop.
The car can eat and drink.
He has eyes, arms and legs.
He can walk.
The car can kiss girls.
He has hair.
He can go fast.

Matthew Newby (10)
St Paul's CE Primary School, Preston

The Snake

The snake
Was eating a cake
In a lake
And it's
Raining rakes.

Jake the Snake
And Daniel
The Spaniel
Had a fight
Jake the Snake
Had the most might.

The snail was
Hitting a nail
Into Jake the Snake's
Cakes.

Jake Sherriff (10)
St Paul's CE Primary School, Preston

I Saw A Poem

I saw a poem
Ride a bike.
I saw a poem
Read a poem.
I saw a poem
Go to bed.
I saw a poem
Have a fright.
I saw a poem
Run a marathon.
I saw a poem
Go to bed.
I saw a poem
Watch TV.
I saw a poem
Run like a dog.
I saw a poem
Soar through the
Sky like a bird.
I saw a poem
Go to school.
I saw a poem
Read a rhyme.
I saw a poem
Read a map.
I saw a poem
Float down to Earth.
I heard a poem
Say goodnight.

Magnus McFaulds (10)
St Paul's CE Primary School, Preston

The Tank

Is running to the UK
Is spitting at the enemy
Is in hospital
Is telling tanks about a gun
Is too slow to get home
Is the tank destroyed? No!
Is the tank friend or enemy?

Johnathan Francis (10)
St Paul's CE Primary School, Preston

The Pencil Case

I saw a pencil case at school
I saw a pencil case eating an egg sandwich
I saw a pencil case winning a race
I saw a pencil case tying a lace
I saw a pencil case on a boat
I saw a pencil case put on a coat
I saw a pencil case party like a madman
I saw a pencil case dress up like Batman
I saw a pencil case next to a sheep
I saw a pencil case sing
I saw a pencil case put on some bling.

Luke Ward (10)
St Paul's CE Primary School, Preston

The Pencil

I saw a pencil scratching his head.
I saw a pencil going to bed.
I heard him go *zzz.*
I saw him at school.
I saw him sharpening his pencil.
I heard his mum shout, 'Tea!'
I saw him in the bath.
I heard him go *splash!*
I saw him playing a game.
I heard him go 'Checkmate.'
I saw him at the end of the day
I saw him moving away.

Adam Price (10)
St Paul's CE Primary School, Preston

The Kiwi And His Long Hair

A lot of hair has the kiwi,
  To the bathroom he went
    His hair to shave
      'I cannot do this,' he shouted
        On the bathroom door
          He banged his toe
            Mr Kiwi sat down on his settee
              With his cup of tea.

Chloe Cain (10)
St Paul's CE Primary School, Preston

The Car

The car
Heard Jeremy Clarkson
Was in town
And rushed off
Quick as a fox
To go and bow down.

The car
Went to the bar
Where he talked
To a friend
And went to look
At a shiny star.

The car
Went to a pump
And filled with petrol
He then found out
His friend at Electrol
Had used all the petrol.

And like a mad man
He rushed to Electrol
He went to give him a thump
Like a bad man.

The car window
Was smashed by a vandal
The car angrily shouted
'Oww, what a scandal.'

Louis Irwin (10)
St Paul's CE Primary School, Preston

Different Animals

I saw a drunk hedgehog in the club,
I saw a shrunken kangaroo dancing on my TV,
I saw a monkey doing the robot,
I saw a crazy shark jumping up and down,
I saw a fat mouse in my fridge saying, 'Hi!'
I saw a green fox in the woods, he said, 'Yo!'
I saw a dog dancing in the street,
I saw an eagle break dancing,
I saw a worm teaching maths,
I saw a crazy snake wearing glasses,
I saw a funky duck going to school,
I saw a fox having a party,
I saw a lion wearing a mask,
I saw a green worm dancing on my bed,
I saw a bull saying, 'Boo!'

Ciaran Bonney (10)
St Paul's CE Primary School, Preston

The Tree

The tree
Woke up, swept
Off
Her silver snow,
As she put on her
Silky suncream
She took off her
Winter coat
Put on her
Scorching hot
Summer dress
And danced in the
Sun.

Jessica Turvey (11)
St Paul's CE Primary School, Preston

The Tree

The tree
Swept off her snow,
As she put on the
Soaking suncream
On her bark

She took off
Her winter jacket
As she put on
Her summer dress.

Aaron Myers (10)
St Paul's CE Primary School, Preston

Sadie

I have a dog called Sadie
Who is not at all lazy
And with food in her mush
She's as daft as a brush
My beautiful Mastiff Sadie

Her beautiful fur is soft and sandy
And her kisses are as sweet as candy
She wags her tail and starts to bark
To let me know it's time for a walk
My clever Mastiff Sadie

When on her lead and we are out
She drags and pulls until I fall about
As I fall to the ground I laugh out loud
And tell her she makes me very proud
My talented Mastiff Sadie.

Warren Baynham (10)
Sacred Heart Catholic Primary School, Wigan

Rubydoo The Perfect Puppy!

Once upon a time in a place far away,
A dog nearly died on the fourth of May.
A carriage pulled by, a big fat shire
And ran over the dog, every little tyre.

The kind old wizard from the village,
Whose silly name was, Mr Phillage!
He tried to save the little dog's looks,
So he had a look in, his magic books.

One of the dog's, diamond eyes,
Had to come out, what a surprise!
But the story indeed is not over yet,
As the dog's leg was broken, could you forget?

The kind sweet fairy, on the mountain,
Cleansed the dog's leg in the sacred fountain!
But after all the fuss and commotion,
The dog had to eat her special potion.

The owners of the dog, thanked the fairy,
The fairy said, 'I just stopped her looking scary!'
Now that's the end of this rhyme
But unfortunately the dog, didn't have a good time!

Georgia Milner (10)
Sacred Heart Catholic Primary School, Wigan

The Mermaid Poem

Once upon a time at the bottom of the sea,
Two mermaids were having a cup of tea,
One was called Faye,
And the other called May,
They were having an amazing day!

Then along came a monkey,
Dancing very funky,
He was doing the hip hop beat,
With his dancing feet,
The mermaids were clapping out of their seats.

A big fat shark,
Swam out of the misty dark,
It gave the mermaids such a fright,
Then it all started a great big fight.

The poem ends,
When they all become friends,
They all live happily ever after,
But they all got dafter.

Nicole Farrimond & Ellie Giddings (10)
Sacred Heart Catholic Primary School, Wigan

148

The Little Farm

Once upon a time, on a tiny little farm,
All the animals were nice and calm.
The monkey and the cow didn't get along,
The cow was always singing an annoying song.

On this farm worked a man named Ned,
Who was a little bit insane in the head.
When farmer Ned saw the goat,
It reminded him that he needed a new coat.

All the farm animals had just quite enough,
They escaped but it really was quite tough.
When farmer Ned jumped out of his bed,
He ran after his big, fat precious cow called Ted.

They ran through the shops,
And ate lollipops.
The big fat cow fell over
And that's how he got knocked down by a Land Rover.

Shana Kearsley & Sasha Sephton (10)
Sacred Heart Catholic Primary School, Wigan

A Magical Quest

Jiggly and Adil were magical boys,
And they liked to make a lot of noise.
They were sent on a mission to find a beast,
Or so they thought, at least!

They met unexpected friends along the way,
Then they came across a monster one day!
Along came captain's Blackbeard and Sparrow,
Then put the body in a wheelbarrow!

The boys stopped short and they stared,
Back came the captains, then they were scared,
The captains said, 'Farewell, goodbye!'
The boys said, 'Come back,' the captains said, 'Why?'

'You will get peace, nice people and stars at night,'
Then the captains said, 'Alright,'
The boys and captains got an almighty cheer,
Then they had a celebration and drank lots of beer!

William Watts (11) & Bradley Walsh (10)
Sacred Heart Catholic Primary School, Wigan

150

Terrible, Terrible Teachers!

Terrible, terrible teachers,
They have such different features,
Fat, round, plump and small,
Our teachers have them all.

Putrid, putrid pupils,
There is hardly any loophole,
They try to find oh so many,
To get away from Mrs Penny.

Dingy, dingy dinners,
Their meatball pies are sinners,
It always takes too long,
And soon you'll start to pong.

Horrible, horrible headmaster,
You need a fabulous pest master,
This is a must, he needs to go,
And that's the end of his show.

Olivia Simm & Elle-Lee Morris (10)
Sacred Heart Catholic Primary School, Wigan

Grey

There once was a city that was unclean and gritty,
It rained and poured and so wet all the kids were bored.
Then a man came along,
His name was Bong
Bong hatched a plot,
You see he does this a lot,
His plot was to make this city clean
Even your toes and in-between!
He tried and tried but nothing would work
But the next day he recruited a friend called Turk
Together they tried
But one day Turk tragically died
So Bong stood on the bank and said, 'You're all crying
With howls of dismay, because it is what we've done
To make this Earth grey.'

Jack Heaton (10)
Sacred Heart Catholic Primary School, Wigan

Big Daddies

There once was a chef, who had a big belly,
He owned a 1 star restaurant which was very smelly.
The inspector is coming, 'What shall I do?
I'll shove all the dirt down my loo!'

The inspector was early, not on time,
He was supposed to be there at half-past nine!
The inspector walked in as thin as a twig,
You could tell his hair was just a wig!
He touched his nose and sniffed around
'What is that on the ground?'

'It's just my leftovers from last night,
I did not mean to give you a fright'
'Oh you've not frightened me, you've frightened your health
Have you not seen the germs on your shelf?'
He went into the kitchen and gasped at his rag
'Whoa calm down mate and stop being a nag!'

'Before you clean your kitchen, have a bath'
'Ha, ha mate you're having a laugh'
'Ger up those stairs straight away or I'll kick you up myself'
'Okay I'll have one but don't give up on my health!'
He washed and washed and finally learnt how to use soap
When he finished he walked down the stairs full of hope.

'Wow you clean up well, let's sell, sell, sell!'
Next week there was a knock at the door, it was the inspector
How could he want more?
'Hello Mr Chef, now I've got news for you've got 5 stars!'
'Oh my gosh now I can get 3 new cars!'

Charlotte Pennington & Kori Alya Beardsworth (10)
Sacred Heart Catholic Primary School, Wigan

Natural Disasters

Once upon a time in the country of Bombaster,
All that ever happened were whopping disasters.

Volcanoes erupted every other day,
It made all the people go away.

It was so near the sea the very next day,
A tsunami came and made everyone pay.

One Monday evening the wind was so strong,
A tornado came and blew them all along.

On Wednesday morning there was a rumble in the ground,
It made everyone jump and some made a sound.

The people who stayed there were very brave,
Though one day they may come to their grave.

Daniel Glaister & Michael Winstanley (10)
Sacred Heart Catholic Primary School, Wigan

Journey Home

I remember the long homeward ride.
The old, black chugging train racing like a rocket.
The old stony castle waiting for the sunset,
Not too stiff, not too tall, just right.
I could smell the salt of the sea making my nose twitch.
Fluffy, white sheep eating the fresh grass.
The mountain as tall as a skyscraper,
Snow melting from the sky.
Bluebells rocking in the dark, deep forest,
As hard as they could.
Home at last.

Ellie Parish (9)
Spilsby Primary School, Spilsby

Journey Home

I remember the long homeward ride.
I saw the horizon sunbathing in the sun.
The rusty train rail sparkling as the sun came up.
White robot houses glimpsed with
His miniature eyes at the towering castle.
Home at last, time to lay down my head and sleep.

Grace Conlay (9)
Spilsby Primary School, Spilsby

Journey Home

The red, chugging, old steam train.
The blue bell singing in the distance.
The old mossy branches giving a bird a home.
The waves lapping each other,
With a crash and a bash.
The mountains as tall as a skyscraper.
The day was very old.
I was getting tired.

Charlotte Veness (9)
Spilsby Primary School, Spilsby

Journey Home

I remember the long homeward ride.
I scanned the field for animals.
I saw reindeer and some deer.
I could hear the trees waving bye.
I felt like a stream of hot water.
I saw a big house with an old man waving.
Home at last, time to lay down my head and sleep.

Morgan Smith (9)
Spilsby Primary School, Spilsby

The Journey Home

I remember the long homeward ride.
I saw fluffy sheep
Eating freshly mown grass on the green fields.
The trees waving bye to me on the way home.
The puffy clouds making funny faces of my family.
I saw frogs jumping on lily pads.
I saw people getting off the train and into their houses.
Home at last, time to lay down my head and go to sleep.

JJ Hayes (9)
Spilsby Primary School, Spilsby

Journey Home

The old train chugging away.
The train man shouting, 'Tickets please.'
Heading through a dark tunnel.
The sunshine gazing in my face.
Home at last, time to lay down my head and sleep.

Jay McNamara (9)
Spilsby Primary School, Spilsby

Journey Home

I remember the long homeward ride.
The old steam train starting its motor.
Fluffy, white sheep nibbling
The freshly mown, dewy grass.
Past luscious fields growing lovely fresh corn.
The wavy trees dripping like milk in a bowl.
I saw a flowing river with wiggly fish.
Home at last.

Jack Taylor (9)
Spilsby Primary School, Spilsby

Journey Home

I remember the long homeward ride.
With the black, old steam train we set off.
I just caught a glimpse of baby lambs just born.
Birds singing like I was in Heaven.
Dripping green grass.
I saw a blue, gorgeous waterfall.
Home at last, time to lay down my head and sleep.

Morgan Arabin (9)
Spilsby Primary School, Spilsby

Journey Home

The old black steam train chugging along.
I remember fluffy white sheep
Chewing the gorgeous grass.
The forest trees wiggling about strangely.
The sandy yellow beach as shiny as the sun.
The waves as blue as the sky.
The crinkly old castle waving to people going past.
The fluffy clouds as soft as fur.
The rocks on the beach laying like statues.
Home at last, time to lay down my head and sleep.

Owen Freeman (9)
Spilsby Primary School, Spilsby

Journey Home

I remember the long homeward ride.
I saw fluffy sheep chomping the freshly cut grass.
There were trees swaying in the breezy wind.
I remember the pretty flowers in the huge field.
The rocky mountain as large as a skyscraper.
Home at last, time to lay down my head and sleep.

Matthew Troughton (9)
Spilsby Primary School, Spilsby

Journey Home

I remember the long homeward ride.
The train was chugging by gently.
In the distance I saw horses trotting by.
On the high mountain above
I saw clouds drifting by.
I stared at seagulls swooping down to the shore.
I saw a glittering lake shining in the sun.
At last I arrived at my destination.
I jumped off and went to wait at the end for my mum.

William Cromie (9)
Spilsby Primary School, Spilsby

Journey Home

I remember the long homeward ride.
I saw animals and meadows.
Lovely beaches and rivers.
Forests and lovely sparkling water.
Fields of fluffy, white sheep and
Trees blowing in the wind.

Ryan Simpson (9)
Spilsby Primary School, Spilsby

Journey Home

I remember the long homeward ride.
I got bored watching the animals.
I went past the beach and the waves flowing to the shore.
The castle was standing tall and proud in the strong wind.
I went past a lot of white fluffy sheep
And white sparkling bungalows.
I went past a forest of beautiful sparkling green trees.
In the forest I saw an army of bluebells
Flying in the breeze.
Home at last, time to lay down my head and sleep.

Nathan Bryant (9)
Spilsby Primary School, Spilsby

Journey Home

I remember the long homeward ride.
I saw some white brick houses
Glimmering in the burning hot sun.
I could see some birds flying above my head.
The clouds were as white as snowflakes.
The mountains standing as tall as a skyscraper.
Home at last.

Luke Pettit (9)
Spilsby Primary School, Spilsby

Journey Home

I remember the long homeward ride.
I saw some clouds drifting away like sheep in the sky.
I could see big, spacious fields with fat cows.
I saw tall, posh houses where rich people live.
I saw a lovely brown fox staring at me fiercely.
Home at last, time to lay down my head and sleep.

Zachary Boyden (9)
Spilsby Primary School, Spilsby

The Journey

I could see round fluffy sheep
Munching on freshly grown grass.
A big rain cloud disappearing in the distance.
The sun rising and rising until morning.
The old black steam train
Chugging along the dull, rusty tracks.
The ocean sparkling a secret smile.
Churches reaching to the sky as if taking off.
The smell of salt making my nose twitch.
The mountains taller than skyscrapers.

William Jones (9)
Spilsby Primary School, Spilsby

Journey Home

I remember the long homeward ride.
I saw lovely, white sheep nibbling freshly grown grass.
I could see mountains in the distance.
Their white flakes of snow
Like sand grains blown from the beach.
I saw churches reaching to the sky as if taking off.
Home at last, time to lay down my head and sleep.

Ben Santus (9)
Spilsby Primary School, Spilsby

The Defensive Shield

Bravely, boldly gives a shield
Bravely, boldly glides a shield
Bounces tactically before enemies can wield
This way and that, arrows soar high
Some brave warriors suddenly die.
While enemy chariots come racing by
Dramatically two swords clash
Blocking the sword before my man got slashed
Then, tactically the shield bounces back.

But suddenly a man wields an axe
The shield parries the attack
Then in the blink of an eye, the axeman dies
Blood spurts out of the defying Spartan guy.
Then, in honour a trumpet is blown
Battle weary, the shield could pounce home.
Overjoyed, the shield was put back in prized place
And the fighter who handled it was crowned an ace!

Lewis Raine (10)
Stamshaw Junior School, Portsmouth

The Legendary Defender

Gallantly and boldly appeared the shield
Gallantly and boldly appeared the shield
Frankly charged through the battlefield
In his guilded armour;
This way and that he observes the bloody battlefield,

Taste of fear danced on his tongue
Protecting and defending the warriors from injuries
Bravely murdering enemies in his way
As he gallops through the gory battlefield
The victory is his
He is proud of his success.

Lauren Sedgewick (10)
Stamshaw Junior School, Portsmouth

What Is Colour? Asked Maddi

Red is the juiciness of the freshly picked ruby strawberry.
Yellow is the smell of the beautiful saffron daffodils
Growing in the springtime.
Pink is the fluffy rose marshmallows
As they are toasting on a campfire.
Green is the smell of Brussels sprouts
As they are cooking in an inky black pot.
Orange is the raw tangerine carrots as you take a bite
And feel the crunchiness on your tongue.
Purple is the taste of delicious violet mulberries.
Blue is the sound of the salty sea crashing against the rocks.

Maddi Robbins (8)
Stamshaw Junior School, Portsmouth

What Is Colour? Asked Samar

Red is the pain in my toe while crimson blood drips.
Orange is the taste of ginger juice sliding down my throat.
Brown is the smell of chocolate
Dripping down the copper chocolate fountain.
Blue is the thundery sound of
The indigo waves crashing on the rocks.
Yellow is the feeling of the sun burning on my hand.
Black is the colour of the ebony sky
When I hear hoots in the thin air.
Pink is the smell of rosy flowers floating inside my nose.
Purple is the feeling in my tummy when I am angry!

Samar Nasser (8)
Stamshaw Junior School, Portsmouth

The Evacuation!

Whistling rapidly, bombs are landing on lifeless London,
Helpless ear-piercing screams echo the streets,
Feeling isolated, the children are in their worst nightmare,
Bang! Bang! Bang! Within seconds
Buildings were destroyed and demolished,
Patiently, the horrified evacuees waited
For the rusty, old steam train,
As fast as a bullet, the train reached the platform
Just in time for the crying children,
Who were sobbing loudly and trembling with fear
Because of the tall, scary wardens,
Eventually, when the evacuees stepped
Onto the open spaced platform they were squashed
Like a suitcase inside the petite train,
When the evacuees arrived at the countryside,
Their carers welcomed them to their beautiful new home,
Evacuees could still feel the rubble
On their scruffy, dirty grey coats,
In relief they threw themselves on the soft, comfy padded sofa,
Quietly they played games and made photo frames,
With other local children and then played
With some toy aeroplanes happily.

Shayna Morey (9)
Stamshaw Junior School, Portsmouth

Londoners Attacked!

Exploding bombs when Londoners are hiding,
Whistling, the rusty, green train,
Which was carrying evacuees,
Arrived at their destination,
Shaking with fear, the children
Who were upset and angry
Patiently waited for their carers,
During the explosions the dark sky was taken over
With black ash and red fire,
Millions of people locked themselves in their houses
And shut their windows, parents broken hearted
While trying to keep their children safe, but failed,
After the bombing, left the people who survived,
Who could see burnt houses,
Destroyed shops and an uninhabitable place to live,
Approximately one month later
The people who survived felt relieved!

Abby Ryan (9)
Stamshaw Junior School, Portsmouth

The Magic Box
(Based on 'Magic Box' by Kit Wright)

I will put in the box . . .
A magical marshmallow football
An evil shark searching for his prey
A burning sun lighting up the box.

I will put in the box . . .
3 wishes that will come true
A melting snowman with a rumbling belly
A shimmering rainbow in each corner.

My box is made from chocolate and cheese
I shall play football in my box.

Jack Turner (8)
Stamshaw Junior School, Portsmouth

The Magic Box
(Based on 'Magic Box' by Kit Wright)

In my box will be
A candy city full of colour
Everyone is happy
A lolly ten feet tall
That towers over me.

In my box will be
Magic adventures through every single door
Like a garden that never ends
And an animal castle
And through one door are two suns and three moons
Amazing horses that gallop on the golden sand.

In my box will be
A fairy tale land
With every fairy tale that you can think of
A mixed-up world that no one understands
And a chest with fairy dust inside.
A palace with a secret wish inside

And lastly my box looks like a normal old box
Because then no one will know it's magic
But me.

Dani Turner (8)
Stamshaw Junior School, Portsmouth

The Magic Box
(Based on 'Magic Box' by Kit Wright)

I will put in the box . . .
A red raging shark
A glimmering golden goldfish
A magic football that grants wishes.

I will put in the box . . .
Rainbow-coloured people
A mum that can change into anything
Fish superheroes.

Josh Addiscott (7)
Stamshaw Junior School, Portsmouth

I've Got Competition!

I'm trying to write a poem, to win a competition,
The only trouble is, I've got a little kitten.
You might think how strange, what could a kitten do
To stop me writing my poem
Well, I will tell you -

He chases at my pencil,
As it moves across the page
To try and write just one word
Can really take an age!
But to tell the truth I don't really mind
You see I love my kitten
He's the best that you could find.

Daniel Cooper (9)
Warbstow Community Primary School, Launceston

The Sea

The sea will crash,
The sea will smash,
The waves will wash,
The waves will rise,
The sand will build a great sandcastle,
The sand will face the mighty sea,
The sea will bash
The waves will dash
The sandcastle will slip away
The sea has conquered the sand today.

Isabel Sobey (9)
Warbstow Community Primary School, Launceston

The Great Storm

A lighthouse standing to attention
Casts an almighty shadow
Across the sapphire sea

Higgledy-piggledy houses
Huddle together
Against the howling wind

Away in the distance
A captain leads his crew
Into the midnight sea

A seagull nicks a chip
From a toddler not concentrating
On her plate of chips

Crabs scuttle to their shelter
Away from the gloomy clouds
Gathering to form a great storm

Crash!
A rumble of thunder
Comes bursting out of a cloud
The first few drops of rain
Come tumbling down

I think I'll finish my fish and chips
Then go back inside.

Sascha Mees (8)
Warbstow Community Primary School, Launceston

The Deep, Dark Woods

Twigs snapping
Bushes rustling
Wind howling
Trees whistling
Moon shining
Children trembling!
Storm coming
Clouds clumping
Trees falling
Children dashing
Mist floating
Owls hooting
Campfire burning
Sausages sizzling
Marshmallows turning
Night-time camping
My friends and me
In the deep, dark woods.

Charlotte Clemens (11)
Warbstow Community Primary School, Launceston

Strangles Bay

Crabs scuttling across the golden sand.
Making their way to the rock pools below
Seaweed scattered in the shape of a mermaid
Coming alive and swimming away

Waves crashing into the bay
Onto the pebbles,
Shimmering like silver in the summery sun.

Seagulls screaming in my ear,
Waiting for me to eat my lunch.
'Not today,' I say
'This is my picnic on Strangles Bay.'

Emily Clemens (8)
Warbstow Community Primary School, Launceston

Not Now! Not Ever!

I will never eat the peas on my plate
Not now, not ever!
You can't trick me, I'm not foolish, I'm clever.
Mum did you know I've got a pea phobia?
I can't eat peas
I'll come out with big red spots called peagrossia!
I'll be ill for weeks or more!
I might turn into a green ogre and roar!
If you like peas you must be mad!
Peas are truly bad!
If I eat a pea I shall surely die!
I'd much prefer to eat a pie.
I will never eat a pea.
Even if it means I will miss out on tea.
Not now! Not ever!

Daphne Xulu (9)
Warbstow Community Primary School, Launceston

YOUNG WRITERS INFORMATION

We hope you have enjoyed reading this
book - and that you will continue to enjoy it
in the coming years.

If you like reading and writing poetry drop
us a line, or give us a call, and we'll send
you a free information pack.

Alternatively, if you would like to order further
copies of this book or any of our other titles,
then please give us a call or log onto our
website at www.youngwriters.co.uk.

Young Writers Information
Remus House
Coltsfoot Drive
Peterborough
PE2 9BF
Tel: (01733) 890066
Fax: (01733) 313524

Email: info@youngwriters.co.uk

SHAKESPEARE QUIZ ANSWERS

1. Stratford-upon-Avon 2. Romeo and Juliet 3. James I 4. 18 5. The Tempest 6. Regan, Cordelia and Goneril 7. His wife 8. Venice 9. All's Well That Ends Well, As You Like It, The Comedy of Errors, Cymbeline, Love's Labour's Lost, Measure for Measure, The Merchant of Venice, The Merry Wives of Windsor, A Midsummer Night's Dream, Much Ado About Nothing, Pericles - Prince of Tyre, The Taming of the Shrew, The Tempest, Twelfth Night, The Two Gentlemen of Verona, Troilus & Cressida, The Winter's Tale 10. Henry V 11. Claire Danes 12. Macbeth 13. Hamlet 14. Sonnet